Shopping over 2

Kays
of
Worcester

Bernard Mills
Oct 06

A pictorial history of the mail order company

by

Bernard Mills

FLAG Publishing Ltd

Kays of Worcester

Copyright 2003 © Bernard Mills

First Published December 2003

British Library Cataloguing in Publication Data
A catalogue record of this book is available from the British Library

ISBN   0-9546662-0-8

Published by:
FLAG Publishing Ltd
St Mary's Close
Kempsey
Worcester
WR5 3JX

Web: www.flag-publishing.co.uk
E-mail: enquiries@flag-publishing.co.uk

Printed by
Goodman Baylis Ltd,
London Road
Worcester
WR5 2JH

INTRODUCTION

The concept for writing a book on the history of Kay & Co. Ltd. started in my mind many years ago when, in 1973, I was first employed by the company working from their offices in Worcester. The whole idea behind this book is to publish, for the first time, a pictorial history of the company covering its humble beginnings, which can be traced back to the late eighteenth century, to the end of the twentieth century. In the past, a number of attempts have been made to document this fascinating history but these have normally been for publication within the company or distributed for public relations purposes to agents, and unlike this book, these documents have never been formally published and made available to a wider audience.

It was my first visit, in the mid 1970's, to one of the other locations that the company operated around the country was that started a quest that is still not finished. If my memory is correct it was to the Leeds Office that I was taken by one of my senior colleagues in order to assist him with one of his projects. I was a trainee at the time and needed the experience but what the project was I have long since forgotten. What I do recall at the time was being impressed by the loyalty and devotion that the employees at Leeds showed to the company. This was not unusual or unique to Leeds staff however. As I gained more experience and travelled more widely many of the employees that I got to know well during my employment at Kays displayed similar traits. Some having only ever worked for the company (apart, in some cases, to carry out National Service) since leaving school and had been employed by the company for many years, or as the saying goes "as Man and Boy". Some were very justifiably proud of their length of service to the company and, which to me as a young man in his twenties, was longer than I had been alive at that time.

What struck me as a little odd as I spoke to more and more people were the apparent contradictions of the "facts" that were given to me about the company and its origins. This awoke my curiosity and started me on a road of discovery and investigation that I am still on. I wanted to discover more and determine the truth of how the company came to be; who founded it and so on. There also appeared to be many "urban legends" that existed about Kays and these also need to be researched so that they could be either be confirmed or quashed. As a result I started to collect together documents, artifacts and make notes on what I was told. These records have now enabled me to collate some of the company's history together in this book.

In compiling this brief history of Kay & Co Ltd, I have had to blend biographical research into the life and times of William Kilbourne Kay, the founder of the company, with historical research into the social and economic life of the company through the memories of its employees, both past and present, as well as the documents and records that exist and the archives that are now owned and preserved for posterity by the Kays Heritage Group. However there are still many areas of research into the history of the company that need to be investigated. As with most historical research, which can always be added to as new information comes to light and can therefore be deemed not to be wholly accurate at the time of publication, please accept, in advance, any mistakes in accuracy that are made in the narrative in this book. If, as a reader of this work, you can add to the knowledge of Kays from personal memories, documents in your possession, photographs and so on then please contact the publishers at the address at the beginning of the book. If you know of someone who can add to this knowledge then please put him or her in contact with me through the publishers.

What is contained within this book is a summary of the knowledge and known facts about Kays and I have deliberately concentrated on the development of the company in Worcester. I do recognise that each of the office and warehouse locations that the company operated will have their own stories to tell and these must be documented for the posterity. I sincerely hope that my colleagues from the offices in Glasgow, Bristol, Newtown, York, Lancaster, Leeds, and Bradford will read this book and help me to add to the knowledge of Kays so that the definitive history of the people and places can be written. There are also those who may have worked for the company in one of those associated companies that Kays operated such as Morse's of Swindon, Attwood's of Kidderminster, Bainbridge's of Lincoln and so on.

It is unusual to produce a "biography" on a company as this field of writing is normally reserved for the famous, either living or dead. Kays is a living organisation that has existed for over two hundred years and its life story continues today. It is the stories of the people who worked at Kays and their memories that must be recorded and preserved for the future generations to enjoy.

Bernard Mills
Worcester
November 2003

Kay & Co Ltd
A brief history of the mail-order company

The city of Worcester has developed along the east and west banks of the River Severn since Roman times. Worcester's magnificent Norman Cathedral dominates the view from the banks of the river. It is a city steeped in history and tradition and was, at one time, one of the most important cities in England.

Worcester is in many ways the typical English provincial city with its development of industry and commerce co-existing with the rural economy and the countryside. As a city, it is still the home of several well-known enterprises such as the Royal Worcester Porcelain Works, Lea & Perrins' Worcestershire Sauce and the oldest newspaper in the world, the Berrow's Worcester Journal.

The birthplace of the famous English composer, Sir Edward Elgar, is close by at Lower Broadheath. The springs that supply Malvern Water to the world are also close by, as the Malvern Hills are on the western boundary of Worcestershire County and are visible from the city (on a clear day).

Worcester was for many years also the headquarters and centre of operations of the largest, and perhaps the oldest, mail-order company in Britain – Kay & Co Ltd. To document and write the history of Kays, as a business is to take a trip through the development of what is, today, referred to as the consumer society. It is a history of shopping over 200 years.

In 1886, a young man made a life changing decision that would not only affect him and his family but ultimately the economic and social culture of the whole country. His name was William Kilbourne Kay and he founded the company that is now known as Kay & Co Ltd.

Originally from Market Harborough in Leicestershire, Kay appears to have come to Worcester as a young man. An established jeweller and watchmaker by the name of John Martin Skarratt employed him. Skarratt ran the business that his grandfather, also called John Skarratt, had established in Worcester during the 1790's.

The senior John Skarratt grew up in London and was apprenticed as a watchmaker there. He moved to Worcester in the latter part of the eighteenth century but although the exact date is not known Skarratt was running a successful clock and watch business in 1794. Skarratt grew his business from humble beginnings from his shop in Goose Lane, Worcester and he expanded his trade so that by 1814 he had moved his enterprise to larger premises in Broad Street, which is only a short distance from Goose Lane. Here he developed his clock and watch business as Skarratt & Co supplying *the Nobility, Gentry, and the Public in general of Worcester and its Vicinity*.

At some time during the nineteenth century, Goose Lane was renamed as St Swithin's Street and the street is still called by that name to this day. The street is still part of Worcester's main central shopping area situated around the Cross, in the centre of the city. The original shop used by Skarratt can be seen in St Swithin's Street and continues to be used as a retail premises.

William Kilbourne Kay must have felt that he had "prospects" in the employ of Skarratt for he had married his sweetheart, Miss Jessie Farenden in February 1883. Jessie must have originally come from Southampton for they were married at the Parish Church of St Luke's in that city on the fifteenth of February in that year. Kay's *rank or profession* is given as a *jeweller's assistant* on his marriage certificate.

Tom, their eldest son, was born in December 1883 and the address given by Kay on the birth certificate indicates that he was living at number 3 Broad Street, which is the address of Skarratt & Co., so he was literally living above the shop. Although he appears to have been born in the mid 1850's (and the exact date is still the subject of research), this birth certificate is the first official record of William

Kilbourne Kay in Worcester. At the time of his marriage and the birth of his son Kilbourne Kay would have been in his late twenties.

William Kilbourne Kay must have learnt a great deal from working at Skarratt & Co. as there is a record of a jeweller's and watchmaker's business in Worcester trading as **Kay, Jones and Co.**, in the early 1880's and pocket watches exist from this company and are dated to this time. It is believed that Kay formed this company with an apprenticed watchmaker, Mr. Jones, as his first real venture into business. This business appears not to have lasted too long as by the mid 1880's, Kay had either left Mr Jones and started up his own business or Mr Jones had left the company. Whatever the reasons, by 1886, Kay had started a new business known simply as **Kay's of Worcester** and he sold jewellery, watches, and household items. He operated the business from number 4, The Foregate in Worcester and it was here that the company remained for over ten years. By 1891, according to the official census of that year, he was living at 115 Ombersley Road, Worcester with his wife, Jessie, three children and two servants. His occupation is given as a *"wholesale jeweller"*. He had become a successful businessman within eight years of being married and within five years of starting his own company and he continued to be successful throughout the remainder of his life.

Kay would have been actively competing against his old employer but he offered something that Skarratt's never did. Kay offered his customers a catalogue of goods from which they could make a selection, order, and pay cash for the items they wanted. It is believed but not confirmed that Kay may have been inspired by the business operated by Mr Pryce-Jones of Newtown, Montgomeryshire (now Powys) who is recognised by many as being the pioneer of the mail-order type of business in the United Kingdom.

Kay's catalogues were sent out by post, on request from individual customers, but this proved to be a very expensive operation as it was soon realised that not all of the catalogues generated orders. Kay saw that he was loosing opportunities for sales when a customer did not order but kept the catalogue. His business was incurring costs that it could not afford in its early days. He saw the opportunity to expand his business by offering responsible and self-motivated men who wished to be their own master, the rights to sell Kay's products from the catalogues that the company supplied. These men would be allocated a geographic area in which to work and they travelled around their territory selling from the catalogues. They made their living from the commission paid by Kay, based on their sales and takings each week. These men were known within Kays as "travellers" and it was their responsibility to contact reputable householders in their area and sell them the goods that Kay supplied. Goods were only supplied on a "cash with order" basis and therefore it can be assumed that only the more affluent households could afford the items offered for sale.

Always seeking to develop and be innovative, Kay saw that a change to supplying goods through the **Kay's Universal Club** method would revolutionise his business. It would allow him to sell to another potentially lucrative market and increase his company's turnover. It is worth detailing the methods used by Kay to ensure that his business prospered in the difficult times of the late nineteenth century. One method relied on the travellers making visits to factories in the major industrial centres that surrounded cities such as Birmingham, Manchester, and Leeds and ask permission from the factory owners to sell goods to a group or "*club*" of their workers. Each member of the "*club*" would make their selection from a catalogue left by the traveller. The member of the club who held the catalogue was known as an "agent" for the traveller and they were responsible for collecting the orders and payments from their fellow club members. As each week passed each member of the group would gradually pay for the goods that they had ordered and when the total order had been paid for the goods were dispatched to the traveller from Worcester. It was the traveller that distributed the goods to the individual worker in the club and visited him in his home. No doubt the traveller also paid a small commission direct to his "agent" for their efforts in collecting the orders and the monies from their fellow members.

Another method of direct selling was also used for groups of workers who wanted to purchase a pocket watch. Often workers in the late nineteenth century had to provide their own watches, as their employers were reluctant to do so even if the job demanded accurate time keeping. An example of this would have been a man who worked on the railways as a guard or driver. The traveller from Kays would offer a suitable pocket watch from the catalogue to the group or club. What was an original concept to Kay's business was that he supplied two pocket watches from the catalogue to each traveller as samples, so that they could show the members of their clubs what it was that they were buying and perhaps influence them to buy the most appropriate watch from Kays. The traveller however had to ensure that there were at least twenty members in each club in order to guarantee that it would be successful. Twenty members in the club made the calculation of the weekly "subscription" easy. There were, in the pre-decimal currency days, twenty shillings to a pound, so members would easily know how much they had to pay each and every week. For example, if each pocket watch were to cost thirty shillings then the weekly subscription for each member would be 1/6d a week, over the twenty weeks. (The use of twenty-week free credit terms is still part of the modern Kays offer to its customers and is a direct link back to the very start of the business.) The traveller then wrote all of the names of the club members onto a ledger sheet that he alone maintained. This ledger recorded the payments made and when they were made against the name of each member of the club. By being meticulous in this way the traveller could see who was up-to-date or was failing to keep up their payments. Each member of the club was also given an individual payment card on which the traveller recorded their payments. By collecting the money from each member, each week, the traveller ensured that he had the money in his possession to order a new pocket watch each week. Every week, usually on payday, the name of a lucky member was "drawn from the hat". They got their watch but would still have to pay the club each week. This method worked very successfully for the majority of clubs as peer pressure from the other members, together with *the common decency and manners* of the time ensured that working men kept their word. Any defaulter on payments would be *"in no doubt from his fellow club members of their displeasure"* to quote Kay's own words from a letter he wrote to a new traveller. The traveller would also get his commission on the sales each week. It is believed, but not confirmed, that this method on buying pocket watches gave rise to the common expression used to explain buying something on credit terms as to "buy something on tick".

Kay's premises at The Foregate meant that his business was very close to the railway station in Worcester city centre (which is known as Foregate Street Station to this day) so the distribution of the catalogues and goods to his customers was relatively easy. At the time that he started his business, in the mid 1880's, Kay employed two clerks and an errand boy but by the early 1890's he was employing at least twenty people and had expanded his operations by acquiring another building adjacent to the Foregate premises. This was used as a warehouse for the catalogue stock.

As with all successful commercial enterprises the need to expand the operations to fulfil increased demand forced a change of premises. Kay moved his business from The Foregate to a site in Shrub Hill Road in 1894. The building he occupied had originally been built as a railway and carriage works (at the cost of £60,000 in the 1850's), but this business had failed, partly because of the cost of the buildings they had built and the site lay unused for many years. It was in 1881 that the Corporation of the City of Worcester decided to organise a "Great Commercial Exhibition" and the Shrub Hill site was chosen as the venue for this showcase event. The exhibition itself took place between July and October 1882 and was judged a great success however, the buildings at Shrub Hill were not used again after the exhibition, and they gradually fell into a state of disrepair. Kay decided to rent them on a fifteen-year agreement in 1893 and he spent a considerable amount of money refurbishing the buildings and making them suitable for his new centre of operations. The buildings offered many advantages to the company, which by this time was known as **"Kay's Universal Stores"**.

The *"offices and manufactories"* of the company were once again conveniently close to another of Worcester's main line railway stations at Shrub Hill. This gave the company easy access to the distribution network that Kay relied on. The easy access to the railway facilitated both the despatch of orders to the customers and the delivery of stock into the company from its suppliers. Mail order was, and still is, driven by the need to get the ordered goods delivered to the customer as quickly as possible and the closeness of the railway helped Kay to make a real success of his business. In a major change of emphasis, Kay also started to manufacture his own goods for sale in the catalogue as well as warehouse those items that he brought in from his suppliers. His workforce had also grown considerably and he was now employing over fifty people in a wide range of trades, ranging from accounts clerks to watch repairers and factory production workers.

Business continued to prosper and, in 1895, **Kays Universal Stores of Worcester** was incorporated and registered at Company's House as **Kay & Co Ltd.**, the name it still uses to this day. As an historical fact the company is one of the very few companies that maintained a viable business with the original registered name in the nineteenth, twentieth, and twenty-first centuries.

The year after, in one of those strange twists of destiny, Kay entered into discussions with his former employer, John Martin Skarratt, the grandson of the original John Skarratt, to buy the business of Skarratt & Co. Skarratt had continued to run his business successfully from number 3 Broad Street and it appears, as often seems to happen in family run concerns, that subsequent generations of the family did not want to get involved in the family business. So it was with the children of John Martin Skarratt.

By the summer of 1896, the negotiations for the sale of the business, premises, stock, and goodwill had been completed and Kay then amalgamated the business of Skarratt & Co into Kay & Co Ltd. After the contracts were signed and monies paid, no one from Skarratt's family had any further part to play in the running of the company.

In a useful marketing strategy to establish the reliability and trustworthiness of his business, Kay used the amalgamation of Skarratt & Co. to legitimately claim that his business had been in existence for over one hundred years (as it would have been in 1896). This was an important marketing ploy in the troubled times of the late nineteenth and early twentieth centuries. Many reputable companies wanted to convince their customers that they were well-established businesses and could be trusted to deliver the goods that had been ordered by them. Apparently there were many so-called mail-order companies that were no more than moneymaking scams. Documentary evidence exists that shows that some "mail-order" companies were deceiving their customers by collecting monies from them (remember it was cash with order) but failing to deliver the goods. These were often back street offices with grand sounding addresses and Kay was adamant that he wanted to give his customers and employees alike the feeling that his organisation was one that could be trusted to fulfil its orders and commitments. It was the heritage of his company that was something he could use effectively and the name of Skarratt gave him exactly that. It is perhaps possible that Kay may have had a certain level of emotional attachment to Skarratt & Co for that was where he had started his career in the jewellery trade many years before.

There was also another very important and perhaps a more commercial aspect to this amalgamation with Skarratt & Co. They also held a contract with the **Great Western Railways (GWR)** to supply "*clocks, watches and timepieces*" to the railway. Kays therefore became the main supplier for a major railway network with a guaranteed income from this lucrative contract and it was one that would no doubt enhance the company's business reputation. The contract with the Great Western Railways saw Kays employ more clock and watch makers in their factory in Worcester. Although Kays could keep up with most of the demand for clocks and watches from the railway, the company was still reliant on other manufacturers to supply them with the components they needed to assemble pocket watches and clocks. Within the Shrub Hill offices there existed a number of workshops for watch assembly, repair and manufacture that had large Milner safes installed in which were kept all of the precious metals, such as gold and silver, as well as the finished watches and items of jewellery.

Kay & Co Ltd entered the twentieth century as a highly successful commercial concern. The share capital of the business is proclaimed proudly on the company letter heading and catalogue front pages as being over £100,000.

A large number of the items featured in the catalogues were now being subcontracted to other *"manufactories"* in England and Europe, although reading the advertising of the time you would imagine that Kays was a very large international manufacturing concern. A company letterhead of the time states that the company had *"manufactories"* in Berlin, Paris, Locle, Keighley, Hanley, and London etc. An example of Victorian over exaggeration that was prevalent at the time and used by many businesses as a means of advertising their success.

There was a great play made of the "Made in England" mark on many of the items sold in the catalogue and each item was stamped with Kays company name. It was at this time (1902) that the Board of directors accepted that the company should diversify and start to sell "Manchester Goods and Ladies Tailoring". It was stated in the minutes of the Board that unless the company did diversify then it would rapidly go into decline as the competition in the watch and jewellery business was growing. This was particularly true of the competition from the Swiss clock and watchmakers that was increasing. The addition of clothing to the range of goods offered in the catalogue opened up new markets Kays.

By 1907, it was again apparent that the business had to change premises once more. Such had been the increase in demand and a corresponding increase in the amount of administration required to manage the traveller's and customer's accounts that more staff were now employed to carry out these functions of the business. This increase in the management and administration led to a decision by the Board to reduce the manufacture of goods at the Worcester factory. The expansion of the sales accounting effort meant that a new office and warehouse would be needed. Kay was granted permission from his directors to start the search for new and more suitable buildings from which the company could continue to operate and grow.

It was soon apparent to Kay that there were no suitable buildings for the company within Worcester itself and he was now confronted by the choice to either move away from the city where he had lived for over thirty years or find a plot of land on which he could build a suitable new building for his business. During 1906, Kay started to negotiate the purchase of a plot of land adjacent to the St Oswald's Hospital in The Tything, which is just to the north of the city centre. After successfully completing the negotiations and completing the contract for the sale, Kays purchased the plot of land for £620 from the Master of the St Oswald's hospital. The site would eventually be redeveloped into the offices that were to be the company's home for nearly one hundred years.

On part of the land were two cottages, numbers 21 and 23 The Tything, and these lay to the northern edge of the plot, adjacent to St Oswald's Walk, as it was then known. These cottages were demolished and the site was cleared of all existing buildings so that the foundations of the new Kays' building could be laid. Building commenced in late 1907. Kays used the address of one of the cottages as the formal address for their new headquarters and so it became Number 23, The Tything. To all employees of the company over the last ninety years or so the building has been known simply as "St Oswald's".

St Oswald's was to become the centre of all of Kays' business activities and the building itself was designed to Kilbourne Kay's own specifications. Kay believed that the new offices and warehouse should be the most modern and comfortable working environment for his staff as he recognised the value that they added to his business activity. The new building was to include an advanced central heating and cooling system, internal telephone system, electric lifts, and the very best toilet facilities for the staff. Of interest to the modern historian is the fact that no provision was made for a staff restaurant in the plans for the new building. The company closed down for lunch at 12:30 p.m. and re-opened again at 2 o'clock precisely and employees were expected to fend for themselves. The level of detail given to the construction of the building was very high. The Specification of Works specifies everything down to the very last detail, even down to the colour of the sand to use for the mixing of the mortar for the bricks. The architect who worked on the construction of St Oswald's was the same one who designed the Museum and Victoria Institute in Worcester.

Kay had also been given approval by the Board to place a contract for watch movements with a small Swiss watchmaker in the town of Locle in Switzerland. He was keen to retain the links with the traditional market he knew so well. This Swiss company was to provide 10,000 movements to Kay's specification and would deliver them to Worcester over the next few years. This contract was reported as being the largest contract ever placed with a Swiss watch manufacturer at that time. It did however spell the end of watch production by Kays in Worcester and with it the need to employ skilled watchmakers. Kays decided instead to buy the watch components from other watch manufacturers, both in the United Kingdom and Europe, and watchcases from local silver and goldsmiths. Kays would then assemble the watches and clocks under his company name instead. This strategy did however fit neatly into the company's plans for continued expansion.

When it was first built and made ready for occupation in 1908, St Oswald's was some two-thirds the size that it is today and although no photographs can be traced that show the building as it was originally constructed, the letter headings used by the company at the time do show the original extent of the buildings. At the rear of the building, there had been a cottage for the caretaker to live in. It was he who was responsible for making sure that the boilers were kept alight for the central heating system and that the building was securely locked up when not in use. Kays still kept precious metals in the form of jewellery and watches on the site and these were locked away each night in high security safes.

At the time of the Coronation of George V in 1910, Kays had decided to extend St Oswald's by adding an extension to the building at the rear. This meant that the caretaker's cottage had to be demolished to make way for this new building. The extension enabled Kays to further expand their business. Due to the design of the building, where the ground floor is actually some six feet above street level, the windows to the basement (where the warehouse was located to store the items sold in the catalogues) are at pavement level and therefore an obvious target for any thief who wanted an easy point to break in. Kays had cast iron railings erected around the pavement level at the same time as the new extension was built. These railings were designed with the Royal cipher for the new King, "GR", forming the centre finial as a patriotic gesture and these can still be seen to this day around the building.

The start of the First World War in 1914 caused a great deal of concern to the business as most of the able bodied men employed by the company were called to serve King and country. Kay's two sons, Tom and Edwin, who were both directors of the company, also followed the call to arms and served in the Army on the Western front.

There was great debate by the Board as to how the business could possibly survive the dire situation that prevailed during the war years, particularly as suppliers of their catalogue goods may not be able to deliver. Many items had been obtained from suppliers in European countries so it was critical that other alternative suppliers in the United Kingdom were found. After some months spent travelling around the country, Kay managed to secure many new suppliers for the catalogue goods and although the range and variety of goods sold during the war years was reduced, the company still produced its catalogues. There were fewer pages in each catalogue; the quality of the paper was not what it had been before the War but the catalogues still went out twice each year.

William Kilbourne Kay recognised the worth of having and maintaining a stable workforce even during the war years and it was at this point in the company's history that a larger number of women started to be employed by the company. They undertook a wider range of roles and duties, including those traditionally undertaken by men. Readers may recall that it was not until the 1920's that women were given the right to vote but at the time of World War 1 women were treated by society in a way that is difficult for us living in the twenty-first century to imagine. Kays was a pioneer in employing the right people for the job and ensuring that they were properly trained and adequately paid for their work. And work they did.

The company faced many new business pressures when the war ended and it is to William Kilbourne Kay's own efforts that much of the success of the business in the post war years can be attributed. He regularly wrote to each of the "travellers" giving them personal encouragement to do better for themselves and therefore the business. He treated each and every one of his travellers as a vital part of his business (which, of course, they were) and often started his letters to them in a very personable and friendly way. He often reminded them that letters from his office were in the way of a conversation with him and should be regarded as such. Kays never really advertised their products through the newspapers and other media but relied instead on the professional discretion of their travellers and the personal recommendations made by customers.

In 1919 Kay and his two sons, Tom and Edwin, travelled widely across Europe re-establishing business links with their "old" suppliers, who were themselves rebuilding their businesses after the War. Kays also started to establish new commercial relationships with new suppliers of suitable luxury and everyday goods. The buying of stock for the catalogue was, and still remains, a challenge as the fashions of a future time have to be predicted to ensure that each catalogue is as current as possible when its is published. Kays expanded the range of goods on offer to its customers and a review of the catalogues of this period shows the much wider range of merchandise that was available to Kays' customers. Everything from bicycles, "speaking" machines (known as *Kayaphones*, a play on the word gramophone), musical instruments, clothing, jewellery, watches and so on. The catalogue was now a department store in a book.

The business continued to prosper and expand during the 1920's. William Kilbourne Kay was however becoming less and less involved in the day-to-day management of the company that he had founded nearly half a century before. He was by the late 1920's in his early seventies and was suffering more and more with periods of ill health. His ill health, however, did not prevent him from organising a day trip for all of his staff to the seaside at Weston-super-Mare to celebrate his seventieth birthday in 1927. Kay arranged the charter of a railway train to take all his staff to Weston and the engine and carriages were bedecked with celebratory banners and flowers. The staff that went on the trip found that they did not have to pay for breakfast, lunch, or tea as Kay paid for all meals taken on the day. There is no record as to whether William Kilbourne Kay attended this celebration day trip but contemporary accounts show that all who went had a very good day out. Kay was suffering from cancer in many parts of his body and in May 1929 he died at his home, **The Elms** in the Battenhall area of Worcester at the age of seventy-two. He lies buried in the churchyard of Hallow Church, which is to the north of Worcester.

Further tragedy befell the Kay family four years later, when in April of 1933, Tom Kilbourne Kay, the eldest brother and Managing Director of the company, died of pneumonia at his home in Malvern. He had become ill as a result of *"sleeping in a damp bed"* while on business in London and succumbed relatively quickly. His health had been badly affected by his war service when he was an infantryman when he served on the Western Front. He was 49 years old when he died. Sadly Tom's wife of over twenty years, Dorothy, also passed away in the July of the same year. His eldest son, Richard, was appointed as a director of the company in his father's place. Richard remained a director of the company up until May 1939.

The directors of the company had always shared the responsibility for the management of the company but William Kilbourne Kay was really the heart and soul of the business. He was the engine that drove it forward and his colleagues felt his loss. After the death of Tom Kilbourne Kay in 1933, his two surviving brothers, Edwin and Jack, and for a brief time his youngest sister, Clare, were directors of the company. Edwin and Jack were appointed joint Managing Directors, with Edwin being the Chairman of the Board also. It was at this time that the directors once again recognised the need to expand the warehousing facilities available to the company and they entered into discussions with the St Oswald's Hospital to see if three houses at 17,18 & 19, The Tything could be purchased and converted into new warehouse facilities. However due to the protracted time taken for the negotiations and the delays caused by constant reference by the Hospital to the Charities Commissioner, the company withdrew its offer. By good fortune, the Hill Motor Company, who occupied numbers 9 to 10 The Tything, had given indications to the company that they wished to sell their premises and the directors negotiated the purchase of the freehold to these properties for £10,250 in March 1930.

As often seems to happen in family run businesses there appears to have been little or no inclination for the grand children of William Kilbourne Kay to take over the running of the business when their fathers had reached a certain age. By the mid 1930's, Edwin and Jack Kay were approaching their middle age and having raised their families may have decided to take a less active part in the business world and the running of the company. It was the same situation as that with the family of John Martin Skarratt, when Kay bought that business from them in 1896.

The history of the company now takes a dramatic turn. In 1936 or perhaps it was in early 1937, the newly appointed Managing Director of the **Great Universal Stores Ltd**, Isaac Wolfson, and his brother, Charles, made a visit to Worcester on business. The reasons for their visit are not known but anecdotal evidence suggest that when Wolfson saw the impressive offices of Kay & Co Ltd in the Tything he remarked that this business had class and it would be the type of concern that he would want within his own growing business empire. There is also anecdotal evidence that suggests that Isaac Wolfson walked into the reception at St Oswald's, asked to see the Managing Director of Kays and there and then offered to buy the whole company no matter what the price, and produced his chequebook to prove that he was serious. However more formal negotiations took place that resulted in the Kay family shareholdings in Kay & Co Ltd being sold to Great Universal Stores Ltd. From these negotiations came the agreement that Kay & Co Ltd would benefit from being given *"administrative and managerial support"* from Great Universal Stores Ltd for the next twenty-eight years at a service fee, which was payable each financial year. The contract for the sale came into force on June 1st 1937 and from that date forward only Richard Kilbourne Kay, the grandson of William Kilbourne Kay and the son of Tom Kilbourne Kay, was involved in the running of the company. Edwin and Jack were paid £228,000 to be shared between them for the sale of their shareholdings and debentures on receipt of their resignation from the company.

One of the immediate results of Wolfson's involvement in the management of the company was his realisation that in order to develop further, Kays needed to invest further in additional office and warehouse space to supplement the offices and warehouse at number 23, The Tything. The package of land that had been bought in The Tything, at numbers 9–10, from the Hill Motor Company, included the workshop that Kays had used as a warehouse (this was referred to as the Number 2 Warehouse). It was now decided to demolish all of the existing buildings on the site and build new office and *"stockrooms"* accommodation in their place. The new building remained as number 9–10 The Tything and was known to all staff that worked for the company simply as "The Tything".

Design and construction of the new building proceeded rapidly for in late 1938 the new building was formally opened after the company spent approximately £17,600. Articles published in the local newspapers of the time refer to *"commodious and artistic premises"* and the entrance hall *"brings to the eye beauty rarely seen if ever in such a building"*. The original entrance doors and staircase in the entrance hall were brought from the Blackheath home of Gordon of Khartoum, according to contemporary accounts, and were of seasoned oak. The whole entrance hall at 9-10 The Tything was reconstructed to look like that of the original house.

Unfortunately the new building did not last for on May 2nd 1941, it caught fire and was totally destroyed. It appears from the formal report written by the Managing Director of Kays, George Lodge, that one of many piles of woollen blankets being stored for the Ministry of Aircraft Production started to smoulder and produced thick smoke which could be seen coming out of one of the front windows of the building. George Lodge first saw this smoke as he left for his lunch at five minutes after one o'clock on the fateful Friday afternoon, just after the staff had left for their lunch break. The fire brigade was called. On arriving at the scene the firemen apparently started to smash the first floor windows at the front of the building and in doing so provided a clean supply of air to the smouldering blankets, which then caught fire. The resultant fire totally destroyed the building and all that remained was the brick facade, including the "Gordon of Khartoum" oak doors, the outside walls, and the staff restaurant block. Staff rushed back from their lunch and with members of the public attempted to recover as much stock as possible from the inferno. Unfortunately much was lost in the fire including many historical documents and ledgers relating to the early history of the company and in particular the watch and clock production records kept from the very earliest days of the company. There are many people alive in Worcester today who can recall the fire at Kays for the smoke from the fire hung over the city all of that Friday afternoon. It was one of the largest fires that Worcester had seen. The fire was brought under control sometime around half past four in the afternoon but the fire brigade remained in attendance throughout the night to ensure that the fire did not restart.

Some apocryphal stories are told that a German bomber returning from a raid in the Midlands strafed the building with machine gun fire; others that the building was deliberately set alight for insurance purposes. These are the tales that urban legends are made of but whatever the cause it is also understood from reminiscences from people who were assisting with the recovery of the stock from the blaze that something of a free-for-all took place as those who assisted helped themselves to items of fire-damaged stock such as shirts, blankets and other household items.

The Tything offices were rebuilt after a fashion by the construction of Army style wooden huts behind the facade. These were used to accommodate one of the local Air Training Corps squadrons (No. 187 Squadron) and they used these huts as their headquarters throughout the war years. The Royal Air Force also used the derelict site at the rear of The Tything to park lorries. It is perhaps worth noting that George Lodge, the Managing Director of Kays, was a member of the R.A.F. Volunteer Reserve during the war and was attached to the ATC squadron in the role of its equipment officer.

World War Two saw the company face similar challenges to those experienced in the Great War of 1914-1918. The catalogues were reduced in size to below 100 pages each, due to paper rationing, but they were still issued twice each year and even contained colour illustrations. Customers needed to provide their rationing coupons as well as money to buy most things that were offered for sale. Easy payment terms were heavily promoted, having been introduced back in 1910 as a means of generating more custom. In other ways the Second World War was good for the business and an increase in the number of Kays agents is noted. This is attributable in part to the fact that women were now working in factories while the men were away serving in the Forces. The idea of a catalogue club suited the time and demand for the Kays catalogue remained steady and even increased throughout the war years. It became a shopping method that remained popular throughout the post-war years and continues to this day with most of the company's customers being women. A far cry from the early days when Kay used to instruct his travellers to only discuss business with the man of the house as women were not able to speak about such things!

When William Kilbourne Kay had bought the land from the St Oswald's Hospital in 1906 he had turned some of it into playing fields and tennis courts for his staff to enjoy and use to pursue their sporting interests. Kay, like many businessmen of his time, believed in the "healthy mind in a healthy body" philosophy and he actively encouraged the creation of a sports and social club for the staff. The Sport & Social Club runs to this day and is still active in promoting staff to enjoy life outside of work.

Fortunately the playing fields behind St Oswald's and The Tything did survive the war. This plot of land is reported to have escaped being converted into allotments for the "dig for victory" effort, as it was believed that the land had at one time been the graveyard for patients of the St Oswald's Hospital. As stated earlier the rear of numbers 9-10 The Tything was used as a lorry park and no doubt the remaining grounds were put to good use. What is known is that the area never returned to being a playing field but was converted to a cinder car park after the war and many residents of Worcester may remember that the Ministry of Transport (as it was then) Vehicle Licensing and Tax Office was located on the site in what was an old wooden Army hut. In the late 1960's and throughout the 1970's the site remained as a car park but this was redeveloped into residential housing in the early 1980's.

The immediate post war years saw continued economic austerity in the country but Kays' catalogue business maintained a steady demand for its goods. It was in 1949 that the company sought tenders from builders to reconstruct the premises at 9-10 The Tything. The offices were redesigned as a single storey building and the staff restaurant, which had survived the fire in 1941, was "designed" into the new construction. As domestic life gradually returned to normal through the early 1950's so the directors felt that they could put into place all of the ideas that they had to expand and take advantage of the growing prosperity of the people in the United Kingdom.

Once again, by the early 1950's, it became obvious that Kays needed yet more warehousing space and as a result the company bought an impressive red brick factory in **Northwick Avenue, Barbourne**, which is located to the north of Worcester. This impressive building was originally built during the 1890's on a green field site for a firm of commercial printers known as W. E. Tucker & Co.. Mr Tucker was himself a successful businessman and had developed his printing business in Worcester, having learnt his trade in London. The building was designed by a well-known architect of the time, Mr Briggs, and with the purchase of the eleven acres of land on which it was built, its construction cost W. E. Tucker over £22,000. Unfortunately due to some poor business decisions Tucker's business went into receivership within three years of moving into the Barbourne Works. The building then led a chequered history being used by a variety of enterprises and was even used by the nearby Royal Air Force base at Perdiswell for parachute packing during the Second World War. In 1951 it was available to buy and Kays did so for the sum of £45,000. This building became the main despatch warehouse for the company and was soon busy with lorries bringing in goods for stock and taking goods for despatch to customers. The building was to remain part of the company's operations for the next fifty years.

As it was a time on national economic growth and with the growing spending power of the people of the United Kingdom, it was recognised that those customers in the north of England and Scotland needed an office and a warehouse from which their accounts could be administered and their orders fulfilled. This would give the company a "local" feel and also shorten the time taken to receive, send out mail and deliver agent's orders thereby reducing operational costs to the business and improve the service given to the agents. The company bought an old flax mill, known as the **Temple Works, Marshall Street, Leeds** in 1953. This building was designed and built to look like an Egyptian temple, hence the name, and it had once been the home of a textile company.

Northern and Scottish agent's accounts were transferred from Worcester to Leeds in 1953. However as far as Scottish agents were concerned this was a short-term move as later in that same year an office was also opened in Glasgow. The company rented the first, second and third floors above a furniture shop in the Trongate, Glasgow although the office entrance was in fact in Albion Street. Here the Scottish office remained until the early 1990's, when it was moved to nearby George Street. Unfortunately this office was also closed by the mid 1990's as the business needs had changed and a separate office for Scottish agents was no longer thought necessary.

In 1956 further expansion of the northern part of Kays' business saw the start of the building of new offices adjacent to an existing building in Marshall Street, Leeds from where Samuel Driver Ltd operated. Kays had bought Samuel Driver (and another similar company, Dyson & Horsfall) in the immediate post-war period. These offices are still in use by the company today.

In Worcester, the company negotiated the purchase of a package of land behind the Cinderella Works (the home of the shoe makers, J. F. Willis & Co) in Watery Lane, which is in the St John's district of Worcester. A new single storey warehouse was built during 1956-1957 at what became **202 Bransford Road.** This land purchase also gave Kays ownership of the Cinderella Sports Ground. Once again the company had playing fields for its staff to enjoy and pursue their own leisure sporting activities. The Cinderella Sports Ground was the original home of Worcestershire County Cricket Club until the building of their New Road ground in the early 1930's. The opening of the new warehouse in 1957 enabled the company to concentrate its administration and management functions in St Oswald's as all warehouse functions were carried out from 202 Bransford Road and Northwick Avenue. The Tything became the main agency office dealing with the accounts of those agents in the southern part of the United Kingdom.

The expansion into 202 Bransford Road warehouse also required more managers to run the operations and some of the younger managers from the agency office were asked if they would transfer to the warehouse operations. Many did so and remained in the warehouse operations for the remainder of their careers with the company.

Two years later, in 1959, Kays bought an existing factory complex on the Hampton Road in **Droitwich** for the sum of £68,000 and used this, once it had been converted to suitable warehousing, as a dispatching warehouse for the larger items in the catalogue such as lawn mowers, bicycles and other items that were either too large or too bulky to be sent through the post. It was also here that Kays was licensed to sell wines and spirits, as the Christmas hampers supplied by the company were also made up and stored at Droitwich. Droitwich eventually also housed an agency office. This was opened to deal with the ever-growing number of agent's accounts that were being added to the business.

Growth in the business saw further rapid expansion in the 1960's. Offices were opened in Newtown (Powys as is, Montgomery as was), York, Lancaster, and Bristol. Further expansion of the Leeds warehousing site was also completed with the construction of another warehouse in Marshall Street. The offices in Newtown were, and still are, located in the famous Royal Welsh Warehouse, which is adjacent to the railway station. It was from this building that Pryce-Jones had originally started his pioneering mail-order business in the nineteenth century. By yet another of those strange twists of fate that seem so often to occur in the history of Kays, the company acquired the entire shareholding of Pryce-Jones, then liquidated the company and amalgamated the entire Pryce-Jones business operations under the Kays name.

In 1962 the company bought another building in Worcester from Morses Ltd, a company it had acquired in the early 1950's, and installed within its walls the company's own photographic studio. This building is at Pierpoint Street and it is where the studio remained until the early 1990's when it was moved to the main warehouse site at **250 Bransford Road, Worcester**. The studio provided in-house facilities to photograph merchandise for the catalogues.

The number of active agents grew rapidly during the 1960's. The minutes of the Board Meetings held during this time note that there were 139,000 active agents in 1961. This had grown to 229,000 agents by March 1966 and had reached a staggering 342,000 by the end of the decade, more than double the number the company had when the decade started.

It was in recognition of this rapid expansion in the number of agents and therefore the increases in the demands on the company for the fulfillment of more and more orders that led the directors to invest in new technologies to modernise their operations. The 1960's saw more rapid growth in the company than at any other time in its history.

Worcester, as the centre of the company' operations, was seen as the starting point for the modernization of the business. One of the first and most needed resources that required a major redesign was the warehousing and despatch facility for the fulfillment of agent's orders. The increase in the number of agents had also increased the number of orders, which in turn had also increased the number of returned items. One of the major attractions of the mail-order business was the agent's ability to order a number of items of a similar type for their customer. This would allow the customer to see which suited or fitted them best. For example, a lady may request a red dress in a size 10 and a size 12, but she would only keep the one that fitted her best and return the other to Kays, all free of charge. The company allowed its agents fourteen days to sell or return requested goods. This was known as the approval period or "appro'" to those who worked in the business. So, by default, the more agents there were, the more orders were received and therefore the more parcels were dispatched and consequently the more items were returned. It was apparent that the company needed new warehouses for both operations, as the existing warehouses at 202 Bransford Road and Northwick Avenue were known to be unable to keep up with the projected demands that would be placed on them.

The company started to look at suitable sites for its new modern warehouse complex in and around Worcester. It was a large engineering works that was located towards the western boundary of Worcester, and which was also adjacent to the main railway line that travels between Hereford, Worcester and ultimately to London, that the company decided would be a suitable site for its new warehouse. After much negotiation and discussion the site and its plant and fittings was acquired in 1964 for the sum of approximately £190,000 from the engineering company, Alley and Maclellan. Once the initial design work was completed and permission obtained from the Worcester City Corporation for the building, the whole site was cleared during 1967 and construction started soon after. The majority of the original engineering works was demolished although some parts were left intact, for example, areas known to this day as Bay 1 and the Midland Office, and these were incorporated into the new warehouse when it was built.

A German engineer, Herr Pierau, was commissioned to design the new warehouse and he devised the way that catalogue stock was to be stored, then collated into parcels that would be sent onto agents. This was a major advance for the company as agent's orders were and still are made up of a variety of items ranging across the whole catalogue. The more items that could be sent in one parcel, or collated together, for onward delivery then the less carriage charges there would be to the company. It also meant that the agent would receive most of their order in one delivery and would not have to wait for other parcels to arrive from other warehouses in the country. It was the automation of the collation process that revolutionised the mail order business of Kays and enabled it to meet the demands of its increasing number of agents. This process did however rely very heavily on the application of appropriate computer technologies to operate successfully.

The new warehouse, which is still referred by many to as Pierau in honour of its designer, was completed in 1968. Its formal address was 205 Bromyard Road but by the early 1980's the company had built a new entrance road onto the Bransford Road side of the site and so the warehouse now became 250 Bransford Road. This huge five storey building contained three stock floors (each of over 44,000 square feet), a packing floor on the first floor, goods inwards and despatch bays on the ground floor, a basement for stationery storage (Kays agent's used a great deal of paper to keep their records at this time) and the top floor was the staff restaurant and kitchens. The area known as Bay 1 was used a reserve stock warehouse with pallet racking. The Midland Office was used as an agency office and perhaps rightly agents from the Midland Counties were handled from here. The one part of the original Alley and Maclellan buildings that remained intact after all of the building works was used as the Staff Shop where surplus catalogue stock was offered for sale to employees. When the new warehouse opened it was not long after that the company closed down its Northwick Avenue warehouse and moved the staff to the new warehouse. The warehouse at 202 Bransford Road then became the main returns handling warehouse for the southern part of the company's operations. Although not exactly replicated in the north, the operations at Leeds carried out the same function of warehousing and despatch using the Marshall Street and Temple warehouses and offices.

Perhaps the greatest change to all areas of the company's operations came in the mid-1960's when the Board approved the development and implementation of the new computer system that were to take the company forward into the 1970's and beyond. Initially the computer team was based in the St Oswald's building (23 The Tything) but another team was set up soon after in Leeds. IBM computers were installed at both Worcester and Leeds. The newly formed computer teams created the computer applications that allowed the business to expand by producing programs for warehouse stock control, order fulfillment, accounts and so on. The new warehouse in Worcester was one of the first areas to become "computerized". The processes for order entry were changed as where those for agent's accounts by the installation of visual display units (VDUs) in both Worcester and Leeds offices.

In the late 1960's another office building in Worcester was purchased, this time from British Railways. Built on a site adjacent to Shrub Hill railway station, its purchase was another of those twists of fate that have occurred throughout the history of Kays, as the company had returned after a period of over sixty years, to its roots. The merchandise buying teams together with the publications department were relocated to the newly acquired building that was appropriately named, **Elgar House**.

This move allowed the computer teams to expand into offices at St Oswald's where the main computer installation for the company was located.

The 1970's saw a period of both continued growth and some rationalisation in the operational areas. One of the harbingers for change occurred in 1971 when the postal strike of that year created severe problems for the business. This strike acted as a catalyst for the creation of the GUS group's own transport and delivery fleet, known as White Arrow Express. The GUS group had operated a company known as GUS Transport since the early 1950's and its main function then was to provide company vehicles that were used to move post and stock around the various office and warehouse sites. This company was ideally placed to form a logistics division that would enable the company to deliver its own parcels directly to its own agents. White Arrow Express was, and still is under its new brand name, Reality, the largest home delivery logistics company in the country and now operates from nearly forty depots strategically placed around the United Kingdom from Inverness to Truro.

Kays continued to develop more and more effective systems to serve its agents and it was in the latter part of the decade that the company started experimenting with taking calls from agents over the telephone. This developed into the "K-Phone" operation where agents could place orders and make enquiries to the company. It was the start of the developments that would see the gradual change from an agency type business to a more individual customer orientated one. Call centres were opened up working along side the traditional agency offices but as technology in telecommunications developed throughout the 1980's and 1990's there was less need to have individual call centres or agency offices in outlying parts of the company so the offices in Lancaster, Bristol, York and Glasgow were all closed. Operations were concentrated on Worcester, Leeds, and Newtown. The advent of the Internet has also changed the way the company does its business as customers can now order and pay for goods over the Internet and by telephone thereby eliminating many of the delays that would have happened with the postal service.

During the 1980's closer operational ties were forged with the sister mail order operations of the British Mail Order Company (BMOC, based in Manchester, and these ties became stronger when GUS Home Shopping Ltd was formed from Kay & Co Ltd and GUS Catalogue Order Ltd (as BMOC had become). GUS Home Shopping became the controlling organisation for the catalogue sales operations and Kays as such disappeared as a separate operating company within the Great Universal Stores plc. The Kays name did still appear on the catalogues published by GUS Home Shopping. Some rationalisation of operations took place in Worcester with the closure of the Merchandise Buying offices at Elgar House and the transfer of the function up to Manchester.

In 1994 Kays formally celebrated its 200th anniversary. A number of special events were held during the year including a celebration lunch for invited guests. The company also commissioned a bronze plaque that was to be fixed to the wall of the original shop where John Skarratt had started his business in 1794. This plaque was formally unveiled by Lady Wolfson, the wife of the chairman of GUS plc, Lord Wolfson of Marylebone, and remains there to this day.

It is here that the story of Kays will end as far as this brief history is concerned for the company has changed beyond all recognition since the start of the twenty-first century and the intention of the author is to record the history of the business up until the end of the twentieth century and not beyond. The Kays name exists today as a trading brand name for the Shop Direct Ltd group and will no doubt continue to serve its customers as it has always done. William Kilbourne Kay would, if he were alive today, stare in wonderment at the sheer size of the company that he started from humble beginnings with three staff. He would be truly amazed in the way that the concept that he created in the later part of the nineteenth century has developed to serving so many customers today. The catalogue is still what he stated it should be – a department store in a book. The company can truly say that it has a history in shopping that extends back in time over the reign of eight monarchs and over two hundred years.

ACKNOWLEDGMENTS

This book would not have been possible without the support of the many people, too numerous to mention individually, who worked for Kays and shared with me their personal recollections on the company over the years. It was their anecdotes that helped to enthuse me to write this book.

I would like to thank the members of the Kay family for allowing me to share some of their personal memories of their ancestor, William Kilbourne Kay.

The support of the Kays Heritage Group for the use of their archives and the use of their photographs, and in particular my friends, Nicky Peters, Ann Petersen and Dil Porter for their efforts in helping me to preserve the heritage of Kays of Worcester.

The support of the senior directors of Kay & Co Ltd and in particular, the Managing Director , David Greenfield, who recognised the historical worth of placing the company archives into the care of the Kays Heritage Group for posterity.

I have to acknowledge the support that my wife, Lyn, who has tolerated my eccentricity and selfish devotion to creating this book and has my undying thanks and love for being so understanding and supportive. My children, Paul and Jennifer, have also helped me to maintain a sense of reality and have kept my feet firmly on the ground.

Bernard Mills
November 2003

Kays
Places

The original shop owned by John Skarratt, watch and clock maker, in Goose Lane, Worcester. This is where he started his business during the 1790's. The picture, above, of the shop is taken from the brochure produced by Kays in the 1920's to celebrate over 125 years in business. The lane was renamed as St Swithin's Street, the name by which it is known to this day, in the nineteenth century. The shop still exists today and is now used by a local florist as their place of business.

These premises served Skarratt until 1814 when he moved to a larger shop in Broad Street, Worcester.

The picture below was taken in the Spring of 2003.

In the late 18th Century,
watchmakers John Skarratt and Co traded from this shop.
They went on to manufacture and sell clocks and watches,
in particular to the railway companies. Under the leadership of
W Kilbourne KAY, the business continued to expand and
became the mail order pioneer
KAY & Company Ltd.

1794 — 1994

This bronze plaque was commissioned to commemorate the 200th anniversary of Kays in 1994 and was mounted on the wall of the original shop in St Swithin's Street, Worcester. In July 1994 the plaque was unveiled by Lady Wolfson, the wife of the chairman of GUS plc, Lord Wolfson of Marylebone, as part of the company's anniversary celebrations. It can be seen in the top right hand corner of the building in the photograph of St Swithin's Street taken in the Spring of 2003.

Since 1994 however new research has revealed that the historical details inscribed on the plaque are not wholly accurate. There is now doubt as to whether John Skarratt started his business in 1794. Evidence suggests that he started trading some four years previously. While it is true that William Kilbourne Kay was employed by Skarratt & Co as a young man, he had left their employ in the early 1880's and started his own business which was trading as "Kays of Worcester". It is this company, that Kay started in 1886, which is the direct descendant of the modern mail-order company. Skarratt & Co was bought by Kays in 1896 and amalgamated into the business.

The move to Broad Street in 1814 enabled John Skarratt to expand and develop his business. It was from these premises that he, his son and eventually his grandson, John Martin Skarratt continued to trade until the family sold their company to William Kilbourne Kay in 1896.

Broad Street was also the home of a chemists shop at number 69, that went by the name of Lea & Perrins, It was these two chemists who went on to discover the world famous Worcestershire Sauce from a recipe given to them to make up by Lord Sandys.

The picture shows the shop as it would have been in the mid 1850's as Skarratt built an extension to the premises at about this time and as a result the building was renumbered from number 2 to number 3.

As it stands today as a retail shoe shop, number 3 Broad Street shows the extensions built by Skarratt. Another storey was added along with a widening of the building and it was in these premises that William Kilbourne Kay started his working life as a jeweller's assistant. It was also his home and he probably lived with his wife and young family on the top floor of the building.

William Kilbourne Kay started his business in 1886 under the trading name of "Kays of Worcester". The company also became known as "Kay's Universal Clubs" shortly after this time when Kay started to use his innovative "club" method for selling.

The address of the premises is Number 4, The Foregate and shown on the left is a picture taken from the celebration brochure of 1920. It was from here that Kay grew the business that has became the mail-order company that still exists to this day.

When he started Kay employed one errand boy and two clerks and records from the company archives, show that the turnover grew steadily and more people were employed.

Unlike today however the company only sold watches, clocks, jewellery and household goods.

There was an extensive warehouse (by the standards of the day) to the rear of the premises where the goods available from the catalogues were stored.

The building still exists today and the picture, right, was taken in early 2003 and reveals that not too much has changed over the last one hundred years.

The left-hand doorway has been converted to a display window but the building is easily identified as Kay's original premises. The current occupiers of the building are a firm of estate agents who are handling the sale of one of Kay's offices in the Tything.

After some seven years of trading, Kays Universal Stores, as the business was now called, moved from the premises in the Foregate to the impressive works along Shrub Hill Road in 1893. These buildings were originally built to house a railway carriage building company but this failed as a business in the 1860's.

The building was then used by the City of Worcester Corporation to house the "Great Commercial Exhibition" of 1882. This exhibition ran from July until October 1882 and was deemed a great success by the City.

What use was made of the site after the Exhibition is not known and the site appears to have fallen into disrepair. Its appeal to the growing needs of Kay's business was such that a fifteen year rental agreement was signed. Items for the catalogues were manufactured in these extensive *manufactories and offices*. The close proximity of the main railway station at Shrub Hill made this an ideal centre of operations for the company. In 1895 Kays was registered and incorporated as a Limited Company and the name was proudly displayed along the roof line of the building.

Known to many residents of Worcester as the site of the large engineering company called Heenan and Froude, the building is now in use by a number of small businesses and has been divided into a number of commercial units. This view shows that time has not altered the exterior view of the building and was taken in early 2003.

The wonderful cast iron portico, shown in the previous picture of the building, was apparently still in place just before World War 2 in 1939. No doubt the metal and that of the lamp standard shown in the same view were used as part of the War effort. Many railings outside public and private buildings in Worcester were also removed and some have only been replaced within the last few years.

This extract from a letter head of 1902 shows the Shrub Hill buildings and the distorted perspective used so often in drawings of the time. This gave customers and business an impression to the scale of the company operations.

"Outside Shrub Hill at 5 o'clock" is the enigmatic caption to the original photograph that appeared in the 1907 catalogue. Clearly the horses and wagons are waiting to be loaded with the parcels that are going to the railway station for despatch to the agents. What is unusual is that the station is towards the rear of the picture so the horses are pointing against the flow of traffic. This suggests that this a posed photograph to show the level of operation needed to deliver orders each day. It is a reminder of just how quickly things have changed.

The same view is shown below but this is from September 2003 and shows a modern carrier collecting parcels for onward delivery.

This is a view of St Oswald's, or Number 23, The Tything that was for almost one hundred years the main building in Worcester from which Kays operated. Designed and built to William Kilbourne Kay's own specification and was built on land purchased from the St Oswald's Hospital. The total cost of the building was £16,800 and it was completed in 1907. Kay used the architects, Sir J. Simpson FRIBA and Mr Maxwell Ayrton FRIBA, whose other other work included the impressive Victoria Institute and Museum in Worcester, to supervise the construction of the building. When completed in 1907 the offices and warehouses were considered to be one of the most modern in the country. The building had its own internal telephone system, central heating, air conditioning and electric lifts. Known to those who worked in the company simply as St Oswald's, it is a wonderful example of Art Nouveau design. The clock was never fitted to the turret that is shown on the roof of the building as this structure contained the motors for the lifts and the ventilation conduits.

In fact the picture above is full of artistic tricks. Compare the size of the man leaning on the lamppost with the horse in the road beside the building (known as St Oswald's Road). Either the man is a dwarf or the horse is huge, and its master a giant. This was a typical example of Victorian & Edwardian grand thinking. They impressed with tricks of perspective.

The building as it was originally constructed was not a deep as this view would suggest. The extension to the back of the building was added in 1910 which added approximately 50% more space to the building.

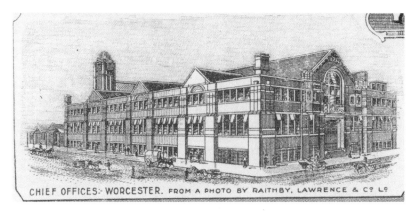

CHIEF OFFICES:- WORCESTER. FROM A PHOTO BY RAITHBY, LAWRENCE & Cº Lº

This print is taken from part of the company letterhead that was used before 1910 and it shows the extent of the original building from a similar viewpoint to the picture on page 45. Note that there are only three "peaks" to the roof line.

The splendid and imposing entrance to Number 23, the Tything. The company name is a very good example of Art Nouveau design. The stairs lead to the reception and the ground floor of the building, which was some six feet above pavement level. Note that the basement windows have been fitted with iron railings to prevent burglary and that the central finials are in the form of the Royal Cipher, "GR" for George V, who came to the throne in 1910.

A closer view of one of the finials of the cast iron railings erected in front of the basement windows during the construction of the extension to St Oswald's in 1910. This was the year of the Coronation of King George V and in a patriotic gesture to the new King, Kays had the railings designed to commemorate the Coronation.

This is one of the few catalogue covers that was produced showing one of Kays' buildings. The drawing is an accurate representation of the front entrance to St Oswald's but in yet another example of over exaggeration of perspective the model seems to almost fill the entrance. She would have to be over fourteen feet tall to do so!!
Compare this with the view of the entrance on the previous page.

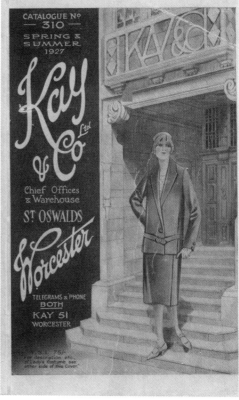

This is a view of the rear entrance to Number 23, The Tything taken in 1982. The extension to the building, that was built in 1910, can be seen clearly for it extends from the "chimney" back towards the rear wall.

By the time this picture was taken St Oswald's had become the base of the Computer Operations for the company with programmers, analysts and operators all sharing the accommodation.

This is where the mainframe computer system was located.

Another view of the rear of St Oswald's taken in the 1980's that shows the car park that was built for the staff who worked not only in St Oswald's but for those who worked in the three houses seen behind the car park. Known as the Georgian Buildings these were purchased by the company as extra accommodation for the Computer Planning teams. These houses were, in the past, used as a maternity home and an academy for "sons of gentlefolk".

This is a view of St Oswald's (number 23, The Tything) taken from St Oswald's Road and looking along the northern side of the building. The extension was added from the point indicated by the arrow back towards the viewpoint, as shown. The cost of this extension was almost the same as the construction of the original building. What is apparent is that the extension did not include a basement area as there are no pavement level windows towards the rear of the building. Just visible are the metal grills fitted to the main windows at what would be ground floor level to act as security for the newly installed computer systems (below)

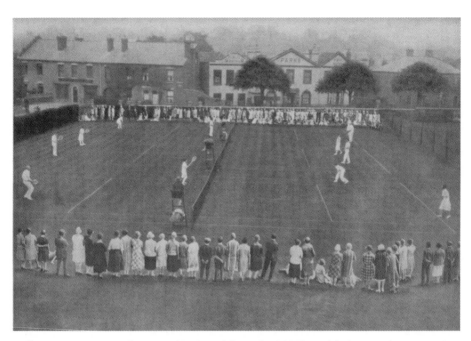

The tennis courts at the rear of St Oswald's in the 1920's and, below ,as they are today.

Views of numbers 9-10 The Tything taken in the early 1980's of the front entrance and, below, the rear of the building.

One of the cast iron lamp standards outside the offices at 9-10 The Tything. These were reported to have been some of the first lights powered by electricity in Worcester and are thought to have been part of the Exhibition of 1882. Each lamp stands guard either side of the main doorway and originally the concrete bases had plaques giving a history of the lamps but these have "disappeared" over time.

The view below of the Tything dates from the year that it was built (1939) and shows the first floor windows and the extent of the front facade. Compare it with the view of the 1980's front entrance. The top brickwork has been removed entirely in post-war restoration.

The Barbourne Works in Northwick Avenue as viewed from the south-western corner of Northwick Avenue and Sabrina Avenue. This picture was taken just before the building was vacated by Kays and White Arrow in March 2002.

Located in what is today a northern suburb of Worcester, the building was originally built for a firm of printers and stationers, who traded as W. E. Tucker & Co, in the early 1890's. Mr Tucker, the proprietor, spent a great deal of money on acquiring the land and constructing the building. However due to a number of bad business decisions, the firm of W. E. Tucker & Co Ltd went out of business within three years of moving into the building. When it was originally built on eleven acres of land, it was a green field site and there were few houses near to the building. It must have been an imposing sight standing alone amongst the trees and fields.

Unfortunately the building led a chequered history after Tucker's failed and more research is need to find out what use it was put to.

It is believed that the nearby Royal Air Force base, at Perdiswell airfield, used the ground floor as a parachute packing area during World War 2.

Kays bought the building as a warehouse in 1951 as their business started to pick up after the austerity of the War and additional warehouse space was needed.

Two views of Barbourne Works from the time when W. E. Tucker originally had the building constructed. The drawing below does exaggerate the perspective of the building and the apparent size of the structure is obvious. Notice the name of the printing company (W. E. TUCKER & Co Ltd) is embossed into the brickwork at the top of the central part of the building, under the arch. Kays covered this over with their own sign when they bought the building. Kays also extended the building by adding to the "bays" at the side.

Over fifty years separate these two views. The view above of the printers at work on the ground floor looks towards the rear of the building and shows the construction of the roof and the open and light environment it created. The view below is taken from the second floor looking to the front and shows the warehouse in 1953. The photographer would have been in the top left hand corner of the earlier photo.

A closer view of the front of Barbourne Works, with a detailed view of the shield that formed part of the archway above the entrance. Notice that the cipher in the shield is made up of the letters W,E, T and "& Co". Such was the weight of this piece of stone that erosion started to take place and cracks appeared at its joints with the main wall. Kays' maintenance teams puts in steel supports to prevent the stonework falling.

The very appropriately named Elgar House was bought by Kays in 1966 and was used by the company until the late 1990's. Located next to the main railway station for Worcester at Shrub Hill and was originally built for British Railways as a divisional headquarters. Kays had come back to its roots, in a way, as the buildings that were used by the company in the 1890's are literally just down the road a few yards away (to the left of the photograph view). The directors had their suite of offices on the top (sixth) floor on which was also the located the staff restaurant. Views over the whole of Worcester and the Malvern Hills in the west from the restaurant are superb.

Elgar House was used primarily as the offices for the staff who put the catalogue together, such as the buyers, stock controllers, administrators, quality controllers, packaging experts etc. Each floor had a responsibility for an area of the catalogue merchandise and a merchandise director managed the teams that worked on these floors.

The fifth floor was men's fashion, soft furnishings and floor coverings; the fourth floor was household, hardware and electrical goods; the third floor was administration and packaging; the second was ladies fashion and accessories; the first was quality control.

An adjacent building was used by the catalogue production team who worked for Mail Order Publications, an associate company of Kays.

This view of the Worcester Warehouse dates from the early 1980's and gives a good impression of the size of the building when viewed from the approach road in Bransford Road. Notice that Kays and White Arrow as well as Royal Mail trailers are waiting to be loaded with parcels in the despatch bays. Compare this view with that of the drawing, below, produced by the architects prior to the warehouse being built.

Construction starts. In the middle distance is Bay One which remains the Goods Inwards department to this day and is part of the original building used by Alley & Maclellan. In the far distance can be seen the roof of the other building from the original engineering works, which at one time was the Staff Shop for employees but is now used as a Catalogue Despatch warehouse.

The ground floor is being built and the basement can just be seen in the foreground beneath the crane tower.

The construction of the warehouse as it reaches the stage where the top (fourth) floor is about to have its roof built. The view above is taken from almost identical viewpoint to the earlier photograph of the completed warehouse that was taken in the 1980's. Both of theses views clearly shows the amount of material needed for the construction of such a major building project.

This aerial view of the entire Worcester Warehouse complex, looking to the north-east, reveals the extent of the company's investment in buildings to meet the needs of its customers.

Key:-

1. Bransford Road Warehouse with lorry and trailer park
2. Worcester Carton Store, built in the mid 1980's, to house the reserve stock. This is a high technology warehouse operated by computer controlled "picking" cranes.
3. Cinderella Playing Fields and Sports Ground.
4. 202 Bransford Road where the warehouse that handles customer returns is located. This was built by Kays in the mid 1950's as a despatch warehouse.
5. The Cinderella Works, once the home of J.F. Willis, shoemakers, but is now the headquarters of an associated company of Kays, Morses Ltd.
6. The main railway line from Hereford to Worcester and then to London.

The Worcester Warehouse looking to the north-west and showing the approach road built in the early 1980's from the Bransford Road.
Key:-
1. Original Alley & Maclellan building that was for many years the Staff Shop and is now a catalogue despatch warehouse.
2. Another original building from Alley & Maclellean which is known as Bay 1 and is the goods inwards for the warehouse and carton store.
3. The Bransford Road from which the warehouse gets its name. The approach road was built to replace the original entrance to the site (4) which is obscured in this view.

This is the building in which Kays opened up its offices for the South West of England, in Bristol, during the 1960's. As can be seen from the picture the building narrowed to the front and this led to some interestingly shaped offices. Located in Baldwin Street, right in the centre of the city, it was easy to get to for staff but a nightmare to park for visitors from other sites. In the late 1970's plans were made to move the offices to the Staple Hill district of Bristol but these offices were relatively short-lived as the company decided to close the Bristol offices down in the mid 1980's.

The office in Glasgow was opened in 1953 in this imposing, almost Gothic, building and was the home of Kay's Scottish Office for nearly forty years. The ground floor of the building was originally a furniture store and Kays rented the first, second and third floors.

Albion Street, which was used as the postal address for the office, is the road to the right of the building.

This warehouse was built for Kays in the early 1980's. Located at Sweet Street in the Holbeck district of the city of Leeds, this warehouse is similar in size to the Pierau warehouse at Worcester. The site had been purchased by the company many years before and is behind the Marshall Street office accommodation.

The offices at Leeds are built on Marshall Street and were always referred to by this name by employees. The offices visible to the left of this view were built in 1958 for Kays and extended the offices that already existed on the site. These were originally the base of the company Samuel Driver Ltd, that Kays acquired in the early 1950's.

Kays People at Work

This fine portrait of the founder of the company was used as the frontispiece of the 1907 catalogue and shows a confident and successful man. William Kilbourne Kay would have been approaching his fiftieth year at the time of the photograph. Born in Market Harborough, in what is now Leicestershire, in or around 1855, Kay may have came to Worcester sometime in his late teens or early twenties but he is first recorded as working as a "jeweller's assistant" for John Martin Skarratt in 1883 at the age of twenty-seven.

It was William Kilbourne Kay's venture into business on his own that gave him the ideas that led to the company known as Kay & Co Ltd.

William Kilbourne Kay photographed in 1920 when he was sixty-four years of age. This portrait was used in the "Celebration of 125 years" brochure that was published in 1920 by the company. This brochure was sent to the company's agents to show them how the business handled their orders and the impressive investment made in buildings.

William Kilbourne Kay at his desk in the early 1920's. The original caption for this photograph read -
"Mr Kay's private office, in telephonic communication with every part of the Offices and Warehouse."
What is of interest is the simple design of Kay's office. There is hardly any paper on his desk and the spartan nature of the room is apparent. The "candlestick" phone being used by the young lady on the left of the photograph would be a desirable object in the antique trade today as would the Underwood "skeleton" typewriter on the desk.

Mr Kay's secretary was a lady who married a well known police officer serving with the City of Worcester Police. His name was "Taffy" Herbert and she was called Queenie. By a strange coincidence her grandson is one of the Security Staff employed by Kays at the Warehouse in Worcester.

In 2001 this office was refurbished in the original colour scheme (salmon pink and peach) as Kay would have had them built. This photograph was framed and hung to the left of the mirror beside the mantelpiece as a reminder to all who used the room, which was by then a meeting room, of the heritage of the room itself.

This is a general view of the Hosiery department taken in 1920.
The original caption to this picture reads :-
"Our business in this Department has enormously increased of late years - due to a large extent to the influence of the short skirt and silk hose fashion of the present day. This illustration gives a view of one of the workrooms where tens of thousands of Ladies' silk and other hose are turned out each week."

The fashion for ladies hosiery remained the same from the 1920's until the early 1960's, when the introduction of the mini skirt meant that "tights" became the hosiery of choice for fashionable ladies and they remain popular to this day.

This share certificate was issued for ten Ordinary Shares in Kay & Co Ltd in 1928. Compared to modern day share certificates this is a very elaborate deign perhaps deliberately so to prevent fraud. Authenticated with the company seal, the certificate is signed by Tom Kilbourne Kay and his younger brother, Jack (Kilbourne) Kay.

Kays always returned a dividend to its shareholders every year. Banks and brokers alike considered the purchase of shares in the company to be a very worthwhile investment with a good return.

The original caption to this photograph reads :-

"Example of a "Machine Room" where our Famous "Regulators" and other Clocks are constructed. The Factory is equipped with the most up-to-date Machinery, and is capable of turning out hundreds of thousands of Clocks Annually. It is recognised as one of the best Factories in existence. Our Clocks have World-wide reputation, and this, combined with the fact that the Department has increased year by year, proves their reliability."

This view shows the complexity of machinery used to produce clocks in the early 1920's.

The warehouse, packing and despatch area in St Oswald's during the 1920's. Accordinging to contemporary papers all of Kay's goods were dispatched in boxes, whenever practical to do so, hence why there are so many boxes of a variety of sizes visible in this photograph The same area is shown, below, as it was in July 2003 after the developers had just finished demolishing the interior to make way for luxury apartments.

The general office in 1920 looking from the rear of the office to the front of the St Oswald's building. The central arched window is the front entrance.

What is known of the women employed by the company at this time was that they were all unmarried. Married women were not expected to work and their husbands were expected to keep them and so any female employee was expected to leave before her wedding day. The company was however generous in that it gave any woman who was considered by her supervisor or manager to be a good employee and was accurate with their work, well-mannered and punctual throughout their employment, the choice of items from the catalogue based on her length of service at Kays. This amounted to one pound in value for every year of service. This was the "going rate" at the time of the photograph and the tradition continued up to the 1990's but to a higher monetary value. The "£1 per year" would be considered a good sum of money when most of the women in this view would have been earning between 10/6 (53 pence) and 12/6 (63 pence) per week. Many girls joined the company when they left school at fourteen years of age and could have achieved ten years or more service before they left to get married so the goods would have gone a way to building their new family home with their new husband.

Every women that left to get married was usually interviewed by either Mr W. Kilbourne Kay or one of his sons, Tom or Edwin. From the personal recollections of some ex-employees these were charming and polite interviews from the directors however more robust leaving interviews were given to girls who were pregnant but not married. These unfortunates got nothing more than a moral dressing-down and were told to leave the company and did so empty handed.

The pictures across these two pages show the agent's account office as it was when it was based in St Oswald's in the 1920's. Over two hundred clerical and administrative support staff worked in this area during the day. The desks were steel benches with swing-out wooden stools. Despite the large fan used to change the air, personal memories of staff who worked here reveal that the office was very hot (and somewhat smelly) on summer days.

The views across the bottom of these two pages were taken in July 2003 after the developers had just finished stripping out the office accommodation built for Kays computer teams. The views are from a similar viewpoint as those above and show the roof construction and the six foot diameter fan used to ensure circulation of the air.

The delivery of mail into the company was its life blood. Mail was the only effective means of communication for the company with its agents and travellers and remained so until the advent of telephone call centres and the Internet in the last twenty years.

What is happening in this photograph, which is another from the celebration brochure issued by the company, is that the delivered mail is being sorted into geographic regions by the ladies behind the benches. Once sorted by them, it will be passed through the windows behind them into the general offices.

The postmen are adding to the growing pile of mail on the floor. It would be very unlikely that W. K. Kay would have tolerated such a untidy method of sorting his post and would have insisted on a more business-like handling of the letters.
What is known is that this is a posed photograph and that each of the postmen were paid a guinea (21/- or £1.05) for their time. No doubt the young ladies were asked to wear new white overalls for the photograph.

Just visible behind the roof of the Royal Mail Van is one of Worcester's landmarks that no longer exists. Known to Worcester residents as Park's Puddle, this was the outdoor swimming pool in the City. The building can be seen more clearly on the view of the tennis courts behind St Oswald's printed elsewhere in this book.

An interior view of the Agency office at numbers 9-10 The Tything, Worcester.

This photograph was taken in the early 1980's and gives an indication of the amount of paperwork that was required to administer the accounts of the company's agents. The computer monitors are mainframe terminals that allowed the clerical staff to interrogate the agent's accounts and so resolve any queries on them.

The offices in the background were for the senior managers and were constructed, in the main, by Kays' own team of maintenance fitters.

There are a few details that are worth mentioning when comparing these offices with a modern call centre as operated by the company today.

The carpet that covered the floor was, if memory is correct, an orange colour with brown squares and was made from man-made fibres. The static electricity on a warm summer's day often built up to give an unpleasant shock to anyone walking near to the metal filing cabinets that were used to store and file documents.

Just visible behind the head of the young lady in the foreground is a typical office chair, probably for a group manager as in the status driven times of the early 1980's only managers could have chairs with arms, and it has a four "star" base, which are illegal in today's modern offices.

Notice the simple "air conditioning" fan on the shelf above the lady on the right of the picture and in the manager's office in the centre.

This view shows the Order office at Shrub Hill in 1907.

There is a mixture of men and women working in this office each industrially writing, by hand, letters to agents and travellers. All record keeping was done by hand using pen and ink. It is reported that lessons in neat handwriting were often given to staff to ensure that all correspondence could be read by the recipient.

On the desk in the foreground is a wallet with "Kays Universal Stores, Worcester" printed upon it. Exactly what this was used for is not known but the earliest Kay's catalogues from the 1880's were made in a similar way.

An interior view of the new warehouse at Worcester showing the "gondel" chain that ran the whole length of the picking floors. This posed photograph (the picking floors were usually very hectic places full of staff completing orders and refilling stock bins) shows the method used to collate orders. As the gondel chain moved across the floor at a walking pace the pickers would place items into one of the three plastic "gondel" boxes hanging from the chain. Each item of an agent's order was detailed on what was known as a "picking ticket". This detailed both the location of the item in the warehouse stock racking and into which gondel box the item should be placed. Each hanger from the gondel chain was numbered and each hanger divided into A,B or C for even and K, L or M for odd numbered hangers. As the chain moved down the warehouse, pickers from each of the three picking floors would place items in the relevant gondel box so that by the time the box reached the packing area on the first floor all of the items for the agent's order were (in theory) collated together in the gondel box. This method of fulfilling agent's order revolutionised Kays warehousing and enabled the company to grow dramatically during the 1970's.

Of interest may be the knowledge that the warehouse manager could alter the speed of the gondel chain to go faster or slower from his office. The speed of the chain depended on the amount of orders to be fulfilled and the time of day.

The typing room in the early 1920's. Theses women would have been part of the elite within the Kays' workforce because they could read, write and type and some, it is believed, also took shorthand.

The typewriters are the Underwood "skeleton" typewriters and these mechanical typewriters must have created quite a noise level within this room when all of the typists were busily working.

A close examination of the original print reveals that a number of the typists are wearing wristwatches, which were becoming fashionable at that time. Before ladies had worn a fob watch on their skirt belt or clipped to their bodice by a pin or brooch. Compared to modern day Health & Safety regulations this typing room appears to be rather cramped. Of note are the chairs used by the typist which appear to be no more than a standard wooden dining chair as would be found in most homes.

The 1970's brought a revolution in the way that Kays processed its agent's accounts and orders. This view of a Visual Display Unit (VDU) Input room dates from that time and shows that, like their predecessors, the women who worked in this room sat in straight rows in moderately cramped, but still legal, working conditions. The desks that were used for the VDU operators were especially designed and built for Kays and remained in use for many years.

It would appear from the documents being keyed-in by the operators that agent's monthly statements of accounts are being entered onto the computer systems.

Is it perhaps peer pressure but why are all of the women wearing their hair long and straight?

This is a view of the Cutting Room used for the production of made-to-measure garments. Although Kays did not feature fashion or "Manchester Goods" in their main catalogues until after the First World War, they did however operate a mail-order tailoring service using the name of "The Dreadnought Clothing Company". Dreadnought was registered as a trade mark to Kays and records exist that W. K. Kay fought a court battle to retain its use when he was sued for breech of trademark. He won the case. The origins of Dreadnought are still being researched but Kays operated the tailoring service from the 1890's and "Dreadnought" catalogues from this period exist.

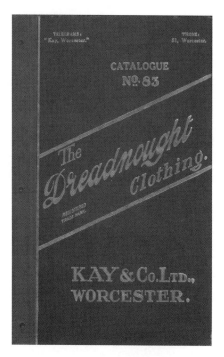

The Dreadnought Clothing Company was operated by Kays for over thirty years until the mid 1920's. The catalogues that were produced were much smaller than the main Kays' catalogue and were literally pocket sized.

Included within the catalogue were drawings of the garments that could be ordered but what made these catalogues unique, at the time, was the practice of including swatches (small pieces) of cloth within the catalogue.

This allowed customers to see for themselves the colour and quality of the cloth that would be used to make the garments they ordered.

Menswear, Ladieswear and Childrenswear as well as clothing for the working man and household servants were included within the catalogues.

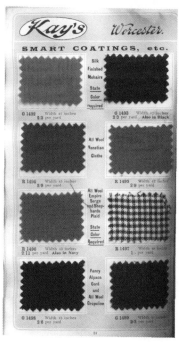

The accounts office in the late 1950's. The quantity of paper needed to administer accounts for the company remained high until the introduction of the computer systems in the late 1960's but was still evident in the 1980's.

The same area of the St Oswald's building is shown below, in a view taken in July 2003, after the developers had moved in to convert the building into luxury apartments.

The Merchandise Offices at St Oswald's, from where the company buyers selected and purchased items for the catalogue. Taken in the early 1960's the picture above shows the original gallery and its guard rails. The void was filled in to provide more office space in the late 1960's but has now been opened up as part of the redevelopments (below).

This is another picture taken from the celebration brochure of 1920. It is a view of the watch factory. There is an obvious need for plenty of natural light needed for this operation as watch parts are fine pieces of engineering. To modern Health & Safety experts this room is full of potential risks to the employees but such legislation was decades away at the time.

What cannot be determined is exactly where this photograph was taken as none of the visual clues such as the position of the windows and the galleried floor above match any of the buildings known to have been used by Kays in Worcester at the time. What is more likely is that this is a view of one of Kay's suppliers, perhaps even in Locle, Switzerland, where Kays had placed many contracts for pocket and wrist watches.

This is a view of the footwear factory. The original caption reads,
"We annually build and distribute hundreds of thousands of Boots and Shoes for the
manufacture of which our Factories are kept up-to-date with the best and latest
Machinery for every department. Our footwear in every section from the heavy ponder-
ous boot used by the outdoor worker to the most delicate shoes that Ladies wear is well
known throughout the country."

This view is thought to be of the Kays' factories at Shrub Hill and may not be
contemporary to the brochure in which this photograph appeared.

The company was sued by a rival shoe manufacturer in the 1920's for using the "Kays"
name on its footwear. This was resolved when Kays agreed to label their footwear "Kays
of Worcester" in order to differentiate the brands. "Kays" shoes are still made and do
appear in the catalogue to this day and are not the mail-order company's own brand.

George Lodge, when he was Managing Director of Kay & Co Ltd, in a formal portrait taken in 1965. George Lodge had a long and distinguished career in Kays and eventually retired in 1975 as Chairman of the company. It was he who alerted the fire brigade over the fire in the Tything offices in 1941. He also served in the RAF Volunteer Reserve during the Second World War as an officer and was the equipment officer for the local Air Training Corps squadron.

A formal portrait of Don Arbuckle, a director of the company, taken in 1965 as part of a series of portraits of the Board of Directors commissioned by the company. Mr Arbuckle was one of the directors of Kays that the author met during his first weeks in the company in early 1973. It was Mr Arbuckle who explained how the catalogue was put together and how the buyers placed the high quality fashion items to the front of the catalogue so as to attract the agent's attention to the offers in the new catalogue.

A keen supporter of rugby, he was President of Worcester R.U.F.C. for many years. Sadly he passed away in January 2003.

(Previous page)

William Kilbourne Kay recognised very early on in his business career that it was important to the success of his business that the money that had been invested in the recruitment and training of staff was money well spent.
Part of this thinking was the philosophy of a "healthy mind in a healthy body" and the creation of the Sports & Social clubs for staff has already been mentioned. Kays operated many clubs and societies for its employees and many continue to exist to this day although there are few that are actively supported by the company.

There were in the heyday of the 1950's and 60's that employees from Kays were involved in football, tennis, cricket, skittles, netball and golf teams that participated in local tournaments and leagues. This is not a comprehensive list of all of the activities that were organised. In addition, staff from the company formed the Kays Theatre Group which still produces a pantomime each year. The social side involving dances and dinners was also very active. It can be seen that Kays provided their staff with a very wide range of activities to occupy them in their leisure hours. This helped people to mix socially as well as at work, and encouraged the team spirit and family-like atmosphere enjoyed by those employed in the company. The company also held an annual fete on the Cinderella Sports Ground for staff and residents of Worcester and this is another tradition that carries on to this day.

As the company grew rapidly during the 1950's and opened more offices remote from Worcester, it became increasingly important that the team spirit and company "togetherness" was maintained so that staff knew what was going on in the other locations. This need gave rise to the Kays internal newsletter which was known at first as "The Link" and later on as the "Kays Link". These magazines contained everything from notices on births, marriages, deaths, engagements and twenty-first birthdays as well as company and sports news. In the earliest editions there were sections devoted to household and culinary tips for the housewife.

The format of the Link changed from the early 1950's, when it was first published as a handy sized booklet to a broadsheet style newspaper in the 1980's when publication ceased. The picture on the previous page shows a small selection of Links from the earliest in 1953 to one of the last published in 1980.

Kays' agents also had a regular magazine, titled the "Kays Money Maker". This was sent out to agents with their parcels and gave advice and guidance to the agents on how to run a successful Kay's agency. It also gave them special offers and that the company had. Often celebrities, such as Katie Boyle, contributed articles on fashion for the company to publish.

Kays Catalogues And Products

Ladies fashionable suits from the 1927 catalogue. The suit on the right hand side is the same as is featured on the cover of the 1927 catalogue shown on page 47.

All items that appeared in the catalogue were hand-drawn by Kays' own artists in the Art Deco style of the time.

No. YE 16.
Price 71/6

No. YE 17.
Price 69/-

These Costumes are fully described on the preceding page.

The goods shown above are cut specially to measure.
Orders cannot be executed under FOURTEEN DAYS

PAGE 15

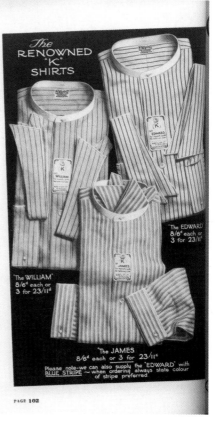

The RENOWNED "K" SHIRTS

The EDWARD
8/6ᵈ each or
3 for 23/11ᵈ

The WILLIAM
8/6ᵈ each or
3 for 23/11ᵈ

The JAMES
8/6ᵈ each or 3 for 23/11ᵈ

Please note-we can also supply the 'EDWARD' with BLUE STRIPE ~ when ordering always state colour of stripe preferred

PAGE 102

Men's shirts from the 1927 catalogue, showing the style of shirt with detachable collars (supplied) and cuffs that had to be fastened with suitable cufflinks.

Please note that special offers, such as "buy one; get another at a reduced price" are not a new concept as Kays were offering discounts on three shirts (and other items from this catalogue) over seventy years ago.

Boys Suits from 1949. Short trousers were expected as were neck ties

Colwer REG'D.

(1) Swing back sister brace kilts in gay Scotch tartan. Both your big and little girl will find this style such fun to wear—and they'll look perfectly charming, too! All wool throughout with plain wrapover front and profusely pleated at the back, fastening at the side with two buttons and finished with the appropriate pin. Assorted tartans.

Sizes:
18 in. 20 in. 22 in. 24 in.
Prices:
21/10 22/4 22/9 23/9
Sizes:
26 in.   28 in.   30 in.
Prices:
24/3   24/9   25/2
No. J.8087.

(2) Delightful All-Wool Bib and Brace Skirt. Cut on the most pleasing lines with a heart shaped neckline and braces fastening at the back. The bib is lined and edged in Red as a charming contrast to the Grey of the skirt, and is also detachable. The front of the skirt is plain and fastens at the side with buttons, while the back is fully pleated to give a jaunty swing. Colour: Grey/Red.

Sizes: 24 in. 26 in. 28 in. 30 in. 32 in.
Prices: 29/6 30/6 31/11 33/6 35/4
No. E.2155.

(3) Schoolgirl's Gym Tunic with steam-pressed pleats. Strongly made in durable quality blue Serge, specially selected for its hardwearing qualities. Regulation style slip with lined yoke and breast pocket. Colour: Navy.

Sizes: 21 in.   24 in.   27 in.   30 in.
Prices: 23/-   24/9   28/7   30/11
Sizes: 33 in.   36 in.   39 in.
Prices: 34/4   37/4   39/-
No. E.2149.

(5) Pleated perfection for your young daughter. Delight her with this lovely skirt which has pleats all round and a wide waist band with button fastening at the side. Crossover braces with buttons at the front give just the right finish to this smart little all occasion garment, in lightweight all wool. Colours: Red and Blue.

Sizes: 18 in. 20 in. 22 in.
Prices: 15/- 16/- 16/11
No. J.8088.

Brace Skirt in soft Wool material. Beautifully pleated all round to give that swirl so dear to a child's heart. Crossover brace buttons to a broad waistband. Button fastening at side. Hardwearing easily washed. Colour: Grey only.

18 in. 20 in. 22 in. 24 in. 26 in. 28 in. 30 in.
Prices: 23/9 24/8 26/2 27/6 29/- 30/8

(6) A Charming Brace Skirt in All-Wool Blue Check. Fashioned in the ever-popular style with plain front and knife pleats all round the back. Crossover brace buttons to waistband at the front. Neat two-button fastening at side. Colour: Blue only.

Sizes: 24 in. 26 in. 28 in. 30 in.
Prices: 25/8 26/7 28/- 29/6
Sizes: 32 in. 34 in. 36 in.
Prices: 31/4 33/9 37/3
No. E.2135.

(7) Girl's Poplin Gym Blouse of neat and practical design. The shirt front buttons to the waist which is threaded with strong elastic. Long full sleeves with one button at the cuff, pointed collar, and breast pocket go to make this the ideal blouse for the schoolgirl. Cream only.

Sizes: 30 in. 32 in. 34 in. 36 in.

No. J.8087.

No. E.2155.

No. E.2149.

No. E.2135.

No. J.8099.

No. J.8088.

Girl's school clothing fashion from 1949

(Utility.)

4 689 New Board of Trade Blouse-type Industrial Overall Jacket. Made from strong Twill with open front buttoning at neck and turn-down Collar. Short Sleeves. Recommended for its washing and wearing qualities. Colour : **White.** Sizes : S.W. W.

3 Coupons.

7/-

(Utility.)

4 690 Bib and Brace Overall in Superior Quality Navy Twill fabric. Two large Hip Pockets and one Breast Pocket. Well made throughout. Ideal garment for work of all descriptions. Waists : 26, 28, 30 ins. **3 Coupons.**

11/6

(Utility.)

4 688 Industrial Coat Overall in strong textured Twill. Cut in regulation style with wrap-over and Patch Pockets. Very hard wearing and excellent for washing. Colours : **Navy** or **White.** Sizes : S.W. W.

3 Coupons. **13/9**

(Utility.)

4 687 Specially produced for Women War Workers. Strongly made Boiler Suit from durable quality bleached and fully shrunk cloth, room-ily cut with five Buttons and button-holes down front and two Patch Pockets. Colour : **Navy.** Waists : 26, 28, 30 ins. **3 Coupons.**

16/10

25

Ladies Utilitarian fashion from 1943.
Notice that rationing coupons are needed to purchase the garments on offer

Beautiful Stockings

Fashions call for Smart Hose and the range listed below offers you practical Hosiery that ensures giving you a neat appearance plus serviceability. All hose supplied in sizes: 9, 9½ and 10 in.

Always state COLOUR and SIZE when ordering.

3/1388
Girls' Wool & Fibro Gym. Hose. Seamless. Colours : **Black** or **Tan.**

Sizes :	4	5	6	7	8
Prices :	3/-	3/1	3/3	3/4	3/6
Coupons:	2	2	2	3	3

3/1375
Stylish and attractive Hose in **Superfine Art Silk.** Fine Gauge, reinforced Ankle and Linked Toe. Serviceable and inexpensive.
Colours : **Vogue, Carib** or **Mistbeige.**
4/9 per pair.
1½ Coupons
3 pairs for **14/-**

3/1376
Fine Quality Hose in **Art. Silk.** New French heel, fine gauge. Schuster finish.
Colours : **Vogue, Carib** or **Mistbeige.**
4/5 per pair.
1½ Coupons
3 pairs for **13/-**

3/1377
Lustrous Hose in luxurious **Art. Silk** of beautiful texture. Perfect slenderizing fit. Reinforced Ankle and Linked Toe.
Colours : **Vogue, Carib** or **Mistbeige.**
2/4 per pair.
1½ Coupons
3 pairs for **6/9**

3/1387
Lisle Hose for service. Excellent quality, comfortable fitting and good for every day wear. Thoroughly recommended for their durability.
Colours : **Vogue, Mistbeige** or **Carib.**
2/4 per pair.
1½ Coupons
3 pairs for **6/9**

28

Ladies stockings as offered in the 1943 catalogue and again requiring the agent to provide rationing coupons with the order.

The Swinging Sixties with a range of Ladies fashion (and one gent) from 1969

5/560
100% ART. SILK MAROCAIN
(Illustrated Below) A gown of real merit designed for all types of informal wear. The style is exclusive and carries a high degree of character. Note the, unusual contrast trimming at neck line, also the pouched bodice. A new feature is the corsage waistline with smocking above and below. Full-cut skirt and all round belt. Colour Black.

Sizes	S.W.	W.	W.X.
Hips	38	40	42 ins.
Lengths	41	42	43 ins.

36/6 36/6 38/8
Carria e 7d. extra.

5/561
(Described below.)

5/558 100% ART. SILK MAROCAIN.
Note the unusually attractive white Pique Collar with decorative contrast. The Bodice carries two delightful Panels tastefully smocked and the contrast buttons are most becoming. All round belt with Buckle and full-cut skirt. Colour **Navy/White** spot.

Sizes	S.W.	W.	W.X.
Hips	38	40	42 ins.
Lengths	41	42	43 ins.

48/-
Carriage 7d. extra.

5/559
(Illustrated Above) The fabric is 100% **ART.SILK MAROCAIN** of excellent quality and texture. Dainty collar in floral Art. Silk Marocain, also piping, buttons on bodice and all round tie in delightful contrast. The gathered bodice is most artistically cut. Full-fitting panelled skirt. Colour **Sweetheart Blue.**

Sizes	S.W.	W.	W.X.
Hips	38	40	42 ins.
Lengths	41	42	43 ins.

52/-
Carriage 7d. extra.

5/561
(Illustrated Above)   Ultra smart number produced in heavy quality **IRISH LINEN** specially selected for its serviceable qualities. The Bodice is cut to denote a waistcoat effect which is most attractive. The high light of this fashion leader is depicted by the Art. Silk Marocain godets in the skirt carried out in Red and White spot. The collar and buttons are trimmed in the same contrast. Colours **Saxe** or **Navy.**

Sizes	S.W.	W.	
Hips	38	40 ins.	
Lengths	41	42 ins.	Carriage 7d. extra.

53/8

2

Ladies Dresses from 1942. Unlike one year later there were no rationing coupons needed to buy these but a carriage charge was levied.

COMBINED TOILET & TRINKET SETS.

We do not now supply these Toilets and Trinkets separately.

P 5301. Toilet and Trinket Set, as shown **25/9**
The Trinket Tray measures about 9¾"×7".

This illustration of a trinket and toilet set is taken from the Spring-Summer catalogue of 1927. The price of 25/9 (£1.28p in today's currency) represented a significant investment by a householder when one considers that a clerk in the offices of Kays was earning approximately 15/- per week.

Before the advent of modern plumbing which brought hot and cold running water to every home, it was common practice to have a bowl and a jug of water on the bedside cabinet.
This simple idea allowed people to freshen up and wash their hands during the night.
The two large cups in the top left and top right of the illustration are chamber pots or "guzunders" for they went under the bed to allow for "calls of nature" during the night.
It was fashionable to have matching candlesticks and all other pieces for the dressing table available in the same pattern.

Kays has a tradition of supplying musical instruments dating back to its earliest days. The Swinging Sixties and the influence of the Beatles on the popular music scene saw an increase in demands for the latest electric guitars and drum kits. The three young men in capes (their mother made them!) formed their own pop group known as "The Daisy Cutters" and performed in the Worcester area. (1964)

mary quant's ginger

1 'THE ZEBRA' - a figure skimmer in dashing White, crease-resisting slub rayon. Sleeveless with a spartan neckline atop a long front zip. A little pleat flares gaily at the hemline.
Sizes : 7; 9; 11; 13.
B.2042 ...... 99/6 weekly 5/-

2 'CHARITY' - on the line in a White baby-doll mini-dress of slub rayon. Lace makes news of the low hipline and edges the gathered skirt. Back zippered.
Sizes : 7; 9; 11; 13.
B.2041 .... £5 15/-
20 weeks at 5/9

Fashion designers have often featured their ranges in the Kays catalogues and this page from 1968 shows part of the range designed by the famous fashion designer, Mary Quant's own Ginger Group especially for Kays.

Kays traditions for quality watches is shown in this picture from the mid 1960's. All of the watches shown are branded with "Kays" name and were only available to buy through the catalogues.

Staff employed by the company and with twenty-five years service were inevitably presented with a Kays watch to mark their achievement for long and loyal service. As can be seen from the photograph there were a variety of styles available for both ladies and gentlemen and such watches are treasured possessions in many families whose relatives worked for the company.

The last known "Kays" watch was commissioned by the company in 1994 to commemorate the two hundredth anniversary of the company. These watches were made by Avia and were available in both ladies and gentlemen's styles.

Flared (and how!) trousers identify this as a fashion of 1977.
This was one of the major changes to male fashion for many years.

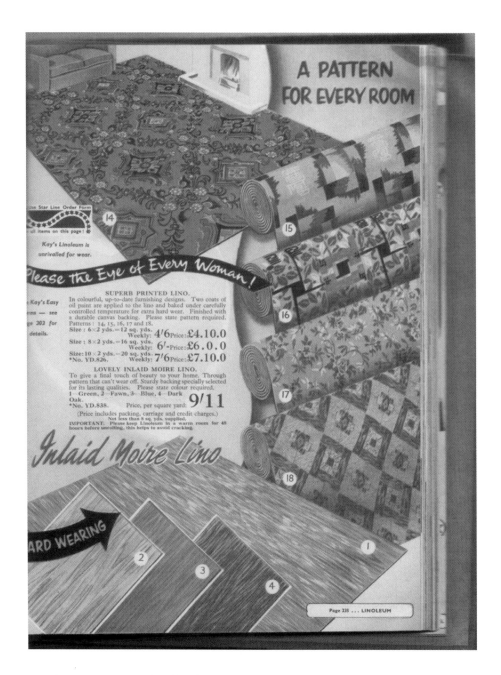

Floor coverings made of linoleum were a must for every modern home in 1954.
It was hard wearing and easy to keep clean.

Celebrity models have often featured on the pages of Kays' catalogues over the decades.
The vivacious entertainer Anita Harris appeared over several seasons modelling her collection of fashion items.
This page is from the 1970 catalogue.

Bob Monkhouse
presents

ANNE ASTON

with fashion specials by **dolly day**

1
MAXI DRESS.
Roses all the way
in posy-printed
Navy cotton.
Length 54ins.
Washable.
Sizes: 10; 12; 14; 16
B.2263
£9.95
weekly 50p

2
PINK DRESS
with tiered sleeves
in burn-out printed
Terylene/Cotton.
Washable.
Sizes: 10; 12; 14; 16
Lgth: 31; 32; 33; 33
★BS.2194
£6.95
weekly 35p

3
COAT AND
DRESS – Orange
and Lemon combine
in a citrus-sweet
cotton and vincel
outfit of daisy
dress and plain
coat. Dress length
33ins. Washable.
Sizes: 10; 12; 14; 16
B.2264
£9.50
weekly 48p

4
FLORAL DRESS.
Black/Multi for
real flower-power
in Dicel Jersey.
Length 33ins.
Washable.
Sizes: 10; 12; 14; 16
B.2265
£7.00
weekly 35p

5
SPOT DRESS.
Polka dot special
in Navy/White
viscose with softly
pleated skirt.
Length 33ins.
Washable.
Sizes: 10; 12; 14
B.2266
£8.25
weekly 42p

Please see page 48
for SIZE CHART

KAYS 50

Another celebrity model.
This is Anne Aston who appeared with Bob Monkhouse as his assistant on the
popular 1970's television show, The Golden Shot.
This page is from the 1972 catalogue.

The kitchen furniture from 1975 typifies the period of chrome and plastic design.

LADY WILDER LOOK

As
portrayed
for KAYS
by
BARBARA
MURRAY...

'The Power Game.'
Photographs by courtesy
of A.T.V. Network.

KAYS 38

1

Dare to wear White when it's
practical in washable Tricel jersey
and versatile as a dress and jacket.
Sleeveless dress has soft straight
silhouette and dramatic pointed
collar designed to show on jacket
too. Belted jacket has buttoned
yoke panel.
Sizes: 12; 14; 16; 18.
★AS.5633 £12 15s 0d
20 weeks at 12s 9d

Actress Barbara Murray played the role of Lady Wilder in the drama series, "the
Power Game".
She appeared dressed in suitable fashions in the 1970 catalogue

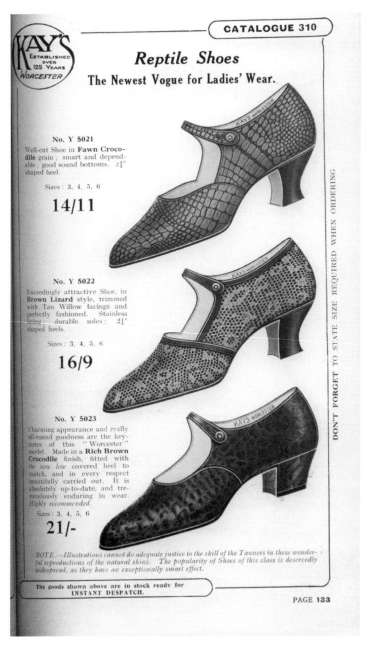

KAY'S Established over 125 Years Worcester

Reptile Shoes
The Newest Vogue for Ladies' Wear.

No. Y 5021

Well-cut Shoe in **Fawn Crocodile** grain ; smart and dependable ; good sound bottoms. 2¼" shaped heel.

Sizes : 3, 4, 5, 6

14/11

No. Y 5022

Exceedingly attractive Shoe, in **Brown Lizard** style, trimmed with Tan Willow facings and perfectly fashioned. Stainless lining ; durable soles ; 2¼" shaped heels.

Sizes : 3, 4, 5, 6

16/9

No. Y 5023

Charming appearance and really all-round goodness are the keynotes of this "Worcester" model. Made in a **Rich Brown Crocodile** finish, fitted with the new low covered heel to match, and in every respect beautifully carried out. It is absolutely up-to-date, and tremendously enduring in wear. *Highly recommended.*

Sizes : 3, 4, 5, 6

21/-

DON'T FORGET TO STATE SIZE REQUIRED WHEN ORDERING

NOTE.—*Illustrations cannot do adequate justice to the skill of the Tanners in these wonderful reproductions of the natural skins. The popularity of Shoes of this class is deservedly widespread, as they have an exceptionally smart effect.*

The goods shown above are in stock ready for
INSTANT DESPATCH.

PAGE 133

Kays have always featured their own brands of footwear as this page from the 1927 catalogue show.
Crocodile or lizard skin would not be used to make shoes today!

DANCING!

No. A.4018.

£5/10/-
5/6 weekly
On Kay's Easy
Terms

No. A.4019.

£8/15/-
8/9 weekly
On Kay's Easy
Terms

EVENING GOWN AND COATEE

The superb dignity of Moiré Taffeta is ideally suited to the larger figure, toning down more generous curves and giving a svelte, dainty finish. The strapless bodice is carefully boned to ensure "stay-put", and features a shaped turn-over cuff set off in the centre by an attractive jewelled brooch. Separate coatee with rolled collar and short sleeves.
Colours: Royal Blue, Black.
Hip Sizes: 42, 44, 46 ins.
Price:
No. A.4018. £5/10/-

NEW BLOWN-ON DIAMANTÉ SPOT

For the night of your dreams! You're heavenly in this strapless evening gown which features a cloud of Rayon net over whispering Taffeta. Scintillating diamanté spots are blown on to the net by a new permanent process, giving a million-dollar film glamour to those with but a few pounds to spend on an evening gown. Strapless bodice carefully ruched and boned. Net stole wrap. Colour: White. Hip Sizes: 36, 38, 40, 42ins
Price: Dress only £8/15/-
No. A.4019.
Stole supplied separately. Price: 16/3

Page 29—LADIES' DRESSES

Glamour for the evening dinner dance is epitomised by these gowns from the 1953 catalogue

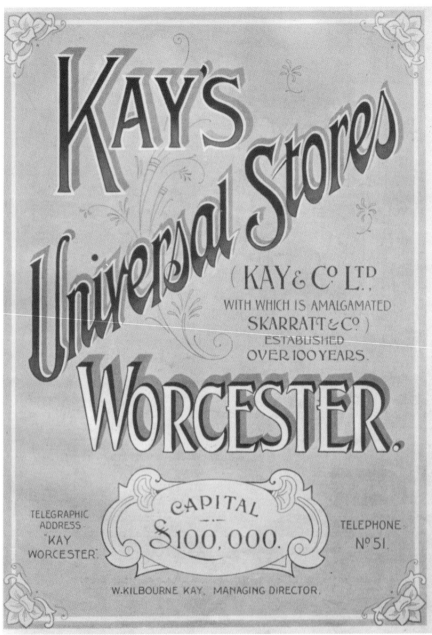

The front cover of the 1907 catalogue. This was printed in black and white and the design was used for several years with no change to the format or wording. The name of Skarratt & Co was dropped from the cover by 1913.

The cover of the Spring & Summer 1953 catalogue features a colourful drawing of the Coronation Procession of Queen Elizabeth II that would have taken place in the June of 1953. It rained on the day!

What is surprising is that this cover was probably painted in the January or February of 1953 but the artist has produced an accurate view of the procession passing under Admiralty Arch (apart from the weather!)

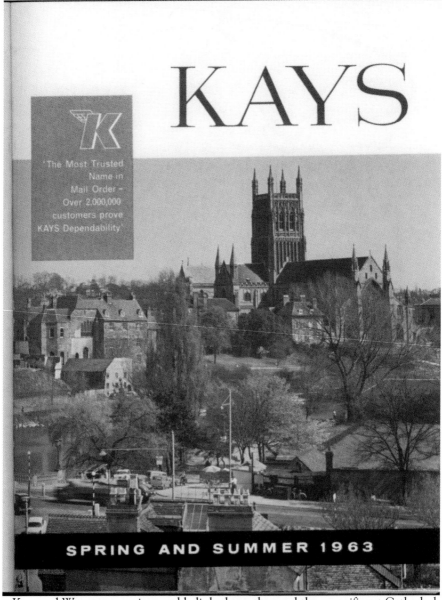

KAYS

'The Most Trusted Name in Mail Order – Over 2,000,000 customers prove KAYS Dependability'

SPRING AND SUMMER 1963

Kays and Worcester are inexorably linked together and the magnificent Cathedral featured on many catalogue covers during the 1960's through to the late 1980's. Either photographs, as in this cover, or paintings from the local museum or especially commissioned works were used.
A similar view of the cathedral is printed on the reverse of the £20 note that is in circulation in 2003.

KAYS

BRITAIN'S NUMBER ONE CATALOGUE
Spring/summer 1983

ESTABLISHED IN
WORCESTER SINCE 1794

K PHONE It's so easy.
You dial, we deliver.
But fast!
See inside back cover
for details

The pictures of Worcester Cathedral were gradually replaced during the 1980's
with those of models from the catalogue.
The new service of "K-phone" features on the cover of this 1983 catalogue.

Paddington Station in west London seen in the early 1920's.
The time is 10:30 in the morning and the train on Platform 1 is the Cornish Rivera Express that took holiday makers down to the South West of England for their holidays.
It was a service operated by Great Western Railways.

Kays had a contract to supply all of the *clocks, watches and timepieces* for the railway and it is highly plausible that the guard in the foreground is checking the time on his Kays' watch.

The large clock above the platform in the middle distance is a Kays clock and was erected by the company on Paddington's platform 1 during 1907-1908.

The clock itself is a triple faced "turret" station clock and was designed and built by Kays.
It was one of a number of designs, which included two and four faced clocks, that the company could supply to the railways.
Kays also supplied similar clocks to city, town and borough councils across the United Kingdom for installation in public places and town halls.

CLOCKS

The largest triple dial clock in Great Britain. Specially constructed and erected at Paddington Station by Kay & Company, Ltd., for the Great Western Company. We are Makers of every description of Clock from big Turret movements to the finest Drawing-room work. (Plans and Estimates free.)

This detail from the catalogue of 1907 shows the triple faced clock that Kays erected at Paddington Station in that year.

The company is believed to have also supplied clocks and watches to other railway companies in the United Kingdom as well as to the Italian railway network.

The Kays clock at Paddington Station, as photographed in September 2003, looking along platform 2 towards the main station concourse.

The view from 1920 would have been taken from the opposite end of Platform 1, seen in the far distance.

The clock still keeps good time but there is no external identification of the fact that it is a Kays Clock as the clock face has been restored at some time in the past and the maker's name replaced with plain panels.

A fine example of a Kays' "office" cloak from the early twentieth century.
This clock was for many years located in the Kays Photographic Studios in
Worcester and is now part of the Kays Heritage Group collection.
It has an eight-day movement and still keeps excellent time.
The face is some 14 inches across.
The clock would have cost thirty shillings when new.

Kay & Co. Ltd., Worcester

Special Watches at Wholesale Prices.

No. A 1601.

The New "Challenge" Lever.

DESPITE many improvements and the consequent increased cost of production, we are still offering this grand Watch at the old popular price.

It has always commanded an enormous sale which has naturally produced many imitations, but our Watch still maintains its lead of all competitors, and purchasers should insist on the name "Kay" being on the dial if they want a genuine 30/- Jewelled Lever of proved merit.

It is a solid fact that this Watch will compare more than favourably with Watches sold at double the price by retail shopkeepers.

Every possible attention has been given to the construction of the various parts, and we can recommend it with confidence as a reliable, accurate timekeeper that will give every satisfaction.

ILLUSTRATION shows our new registered dust-excluding "removable" Cap which completely covers and protects the most vital parts of the Watch from all damage and dust, whilst at the same time by means of a simple device we have made it possible to see the escapement in action without taking off Cap.

We also show the newly improved and right up to date three-quarter plate lever movement which is jewelled in 15 actions, fitted with Chronometer Balance and Stop Work to prevent overwinding.

It is fitted in a neat, strong and splendidly finished hall-marked silver Case with clear white enamel dial, gold hands, and strong crystal glass which rarely breaks under fair wear and tear.

FOUR YEARS' FREE WARRANTY WITH EACH WATCH.

30/-   Thirty Shillings each.   30/-

NO DELAY, always in stock, REGULATED TO A TICK and sent out FIT FOR THE POCKET, securely packed and carriage paid upon receipt of remittance.

283

Catalogue 60.

These pages from the catalogue of 1913 show three of the most popular of Kays watches. The original pages feature exact size drawings of each of the watches. This was a useful advertising tool as the potential buyer could see for themselves how big the watch was that they were buying.

The "Perfection" watch (above) had a long history as a Kays watch having been offered for sale in the catalogue of 1893 and it continued to be sold until 1920. The watch started life as being "Made in England" but by this time was "Swiss Made".

Note that each of the watches was wound, and the hands set, by the use of a key as was common to many pocket watches at this time. These keys were normally attached to one end of the watch chain, or "Albert", that men wore in their waistcoats. Unfortunately the keys often got lost and spares were hard to come by so the watches were often put into cupboards or drawers as they could not be wound up without a key. This unhappy circumstance (for the original owner) has however allowed many Kays watches to survive over time and be available to modern pocket watch collectors.

The New Model "PARAGON" Sewing Machine.

78/6

NO DELAY, always in stock and sent per return, securely packed, carriage paid, on receipt of remittance.

Catalogue 60.

Kay & Co. Ltd. Worcester

Equal to any other make at 4½ Guineas.

No. A 301.
WE DO NOT SUPPLY A STAND FOR THIS MACHINE.

Sewing Machines were always a good and wise investment by frugal housewives, according to the copy associated with this "Paragon" model from the early 1900's.
The picture below is of a similar model of sewing machine dating from the same period. This is one of several machines from the Kays Heritage Group collection. It was "Made in Baden", which is in Germany.

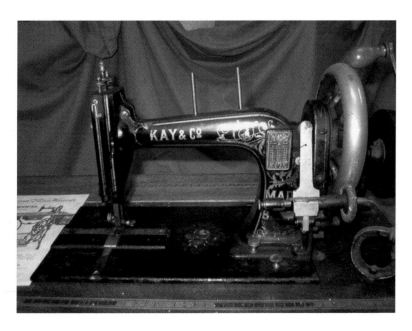

Kay & Co. Ltd., Worcester

A NOVELTY IN WATCHMAKING.

The "Workman's" Watch.

WARRANTED
THREE
YEARS.

25/-

No. A 1608. THE "WORKMAN'S."   No. A 1608. THE "WORKMAN'S."

ARTISTICALLY designed Case, medium size, strongly made in Oxidized Gun Metal, beautifully embossed relief decorations, embodying sentiments appealing specially to Trades Unionists and working men generally.

It has a ¾-Plate Movement of best construction, capitally finished, and accurately adjusted in every part.

Jewelled in principal actions, with specially prepared polished pinions and wheels, hard gilt plates and all the latest improvements.

Sound Lever Escapement with Compensation Balance, ensuring good time-keeping qualities.

Keyless Action, enabling the wearer to wind and set hands **without opening** the case, thus keeping the movement clean, and otherwise reducing the expense of maintaining in good condition.

Strong convex Glass, hard white Enamel Dial, Gold Hands of fancy design, completes this really attractive and unique production.

NO DELAY, always in stock. REGULATED TO A TICK and sent out FIT FOR THE POCKET, securely packed and carriage paid upon receipt of remittance.

Catalogue 60.   292

A watch designed especially for the working man in the troubled times prior to World War 1 when strikes and industrial unrest were common place. This is a true workman's watch from the 1913 catalogue

A Kays' railway station clock thought to be on Worcester Shrub Hill station before the railways replaced the clocks with electric ones.

Maybe railway enthusiasts, who know of other photographic records of Kays clocks and timepieces made for the G.W.R., will be able to add to the knowledge of the author.

This "turret" clock is seen sometime in the 1960's on the wall above the Worcester office of the Midland Red bus company, which served Worcester and the surrounding district.

The clock is still to be seen in Angel Place, Worcester, which is where the main market in the city is located.

First Group, who now own Midland Red, replaced the face of the clock with their name but did not replace the name of Kays.

First Group no longer operate an office from this building having moved, by another strange coincidence, to what was W. K. Kay's house, Heron Lodge, on the London Road, Worcester.

Owned by the Severn Valley Railway, this clock is still operating on the station platform at Bewdley in Worcestershire. The face of the clock is clearly marked for the Great Western Railway (G.W.R.) and is one example of the two-faced railway clocks that Kays would have supplied under its contract with the railway.

Normally mounted on station platforms, thousands of passengers would have watched the minutes pass as they waited for their particular train to arrive.

The pendulum and movement of the clock would be housed in the pillar on which the clock itself is mounted.